Eyes
on
Jesus

Eyes on Jesus

A Guide for Contemplation

Michael Kennedy, S.J.

Foreword by Michael Downey

A Crossroad Book
The Crossroad Publishing Company
New York

Scripture citations are taken from *Christian Community Bible: Catholic Pastoral Edition,* 14th ed., copyright © 1994 by Bernardo Hurault, used with the permission of Claretian Publications, U.P. P.O., Box 4, Quezon City 1101, Philippines.

The Crossroad Publishing Company
370 Lexington Avenue, New York, NY 10017

Printed in the United States of America

Library of Congress Cataloging-in-Publication Data
Kennedy, Michael, S.J.
    Eyes on Jesus : a guide for contemplation / by Michael Kennedy.
        p.   cm.
    ISBN 0-8245-1828-4
    1. Jesus Christ – Biography Meditations. 2. Bible. N.T. Gospels Meditations. 3. Contemplation. 4. Spiritual exercises.   I. Title.
BT306.4.K47   1999
232.9′01 – dc21   99-16158

1   2   3   4   5   6   7   8   9   10   04   03   02   01   00   99

Nothing is more practical than finding God,

that is, than falling in love

in a quite absolute, final way.

What you are in love with,

what seizes your imagination,

will affect everything.

It will decide

what will get you out of bed in the morning,

what you will do with your evenings,

how you spend your weekend,

what you read, what you know,

what breaks your heart,

and what amazes you with joy and gratitude.

Fall in love, stay in love,

and it will decide everything.

—PEDRO ARRUPE, S.J.

contents

foreword

Dolores Mission is one of the poorest churches in the Archdiocese of Los Angeles. Jesuit Michael Kennedy is the pastor of its people. In this land of eternal traffic, four large freeways provide the natural urban boundaries of this mostly Mexican parish. Five gangs stake their claim to its turf. On a recent visit as the parish was readying for the fiesta of Cinco de Mayo in celebration of the Mexican victory over the French at Puebla, I asked Mike Kennedy: "Are the gangs like those seen on television and in the movies?" Without hesitation or blink of an eye, his response: "Much worse. The neighborhood is soaked in blood. A lot of mothers of the parish have lost their sons on these streets."

It was one of those signature Southern California days: a blazing sun's warmth piercing through LA's haze against a bed of crystalline blue; lines of imperial palms providing canopies of shade here and there across the barrios of East LA. Throughout the parish there are Base Christian Communities, wherein the people of Dolores Mission gather for Bible study, prayer, and mutual support and encouragement. On a walking tour through the parish center, Fr. Mike greeted his parishioners one by one, sometimes in English, more often in Spanish. Some were busy about their many tasks, while others seemed to be lingering. Or waiting. Eyes lit up with hope as they caught a glimpse of their pastor.

We stopped by the Proyecto Guadalupano, where fifty homeless men from East LA are given shelter for a three-

month period of transition. Then on to the Proyecto
Pastoral's Homeboy Bakery, where tattooed boys from
the five different gangs of the neighborhood bake bread in
a cooperative effort. A job keeps them off the street. Because of Homeboy Bakery, they have a chance of breaking
out of the gangs.

On entering the eighth grade classroom at Dolores
Mission, Fr. Mike asked the students: "Who wants to
come with us to do the contemplations?" All but a few
raised their hands wildly. The prayer room is on the third
floor of the school. Small and quiet, dimly lit with pil-
lows strewn all over the floor, this is where Mike Kennedy
brings seventh and eighth graders through a series of
contemplations based on Ignatius of Loyola's *Spiritual
Exercises* — as he has done with so many other people
of different ages and ways of life.

Eyes on Jesus: A Guide to Contemplation is the fruit of
many years of experience in the school of Ignatian prayer.
It was during his Tertianship, that period of intense preparation before making final vows in the Society of Jesus,
while in Gloucester, Massachusetts, a serene and once
prosperous fishing village in New England, that Mike
Kennedy put pen to paper in an attempt to offer a descrip-
tion of his own experience in prayer. Informed by the rich
imagery of the gospels, cultivated by the exercise of the
imagination, and nourished through the senses, this is a
spirituality that can be sustained each and every moment
by keeping the eyes of the mind and heart fixed on the
life, passion, death, and resurrection of Jesus the Christ.

Of late, there have been many books written in an effort to make the contemplative experience at the heart
of the *Spiritual Exercises* accessible to contemporary believers. But no author has been as successful as Michael

Kennedy at making the rich heritage of Ignatian prayer available to such a wide range of people. Kennedy's approach to contemplative prayer has borne fruit, not only with the seventh and eighth graders at Dolores Mission, but also with the men of the Proyecto Guadalupano, with Kennedy's Jesuit confreres, with college students, with *campesinos* in El Salvador, with university professors, with the Base Communities of Dolores Mission, with retreatants in Wernersville, Pennsylvania, and Los Altos, California, and with those incarcerated.

How to explain the enormous appeal, indeed success, of Kennedy's approach to contemplative prayer in the Ignatian tradition? First, in the simplest of terms he manages to pass on to others what he has come to know first-hand through his own experience of the *Spiritual Exercises*. But equally important is Mike Kennedy's conviction that, above all, it is Holy Spirit who guides and directs the human heart to participate in the fullness of the divine life. As a result, the university professor and the unlettered mother of a son convicted of first-degree murder incarcerated in Juvenile Hall in East LA can both be led to the depths of contemplative prayer, to the riches of contemplative living.

This little book is a modest tool crafted to serve a single purpose: to awaken the heart to the abundance of the Life that pours itself forth. To Love. To gift. Receive the gift, then, in and through these pages, so that in all things God may be glorified and Christ be all in all.

MICHAEL DOWNEY
Trinity Sunday 1999

acknowledgments

*In gratitude to family, friends, and Jesuit brothers
who have walked with me for many years.*

Special thanks to those who have helped concretely with
these words: Dick Howard and Paul Fitzgerald, S.J.,
for editorial assistance; Hector Gonzalez and Eddy Mar-
tinez for technical help; Wilkie Au and Mary Ellen and
Doug Burton-Christie for inspiration and good questions;
Sr. Edith Prendergast, R.S.C., and Michael Downey for
the right timing; and Gwendolin Herder, who has made
this a positive adventure.

introduction

What does it mean to "deepen" a relationship? In order to get to know someone better, to deepen a relationship with a friend, for example, it is necessary to spend time with that person, to share ourselves, and to try to really appreciate significant experiences the other person has had. It is important not only to hear what the other person might be saying, but to feel the others' words as well.

Deepening our relationship with God is no different. Not only can we pay attention to our own "experiences" in prayer with God, but in Scripture we have the experiences of countless other people, including the biblical writers themselves, to draw on. Entering into a biblical passage with our imaginations and our senses, directly experiencing what is happening there, can permit us to deepen our relationship with God in a way that is unique and special. We can allow our hearts to feel what is happening, and then we can share with God what we feel.

I remember walking one morning through a food market in Ciudad Guzmán, Mexico. The smells, the colors, the variety of food — all these absorbed my senses that day. I was lost in the slow movement of the ladies preparing the food. Before this walk through the market, I had gazed for hours in the morning at all the people slowly walking through the central plaza: students with their books, women carrying their packages, small children playing. They all seemed caught up in the rhythm of the fountain which was splashing slowly in the middle of it

1

all. It was a simple scene, but I felt lost, absorbed in the movement of a slow calm moving, walking around and around the plaza.

To walk slowly through a marketplace in Mexico, to gaze for hours at waves breaking, to peer closely at the faces of campesinos in El Salvador, to speak out against gross human rights violations, to gaze with the mind's eye at Jesus, the compassionate one who heals those afflicted by painful infirmities: What do all these experiences have in common? Where does one begin and the other end? How does the inner journey flow out into the outer journey? What does it mean to be a "contemplative" in the way St. Ignatius of Loyola had in mind?

I entered the Jesuit order in 1966 in Los Gatos, California. It was a transition period in religious life, and my first year of novitiate training was also the last year of the "old style" introduction to religious life. Not much had changed in four hundred years or so. One of the most important parts of the Jesuit novitiate experience was (and still is) the opportunity to make the Spiritual Exercises of St. Ignatius, known as the "thirty-day retreat." Our daily routine consisted of five prayer periods during the day, the first one beginning at 5:30 a.m. There was also time for manual work and for walking, and each night before going to bed, we "made points" for our next morning's meditation. This preparation often included reading a section from *The Public Life of Our Lord Jesus Christ* by Most Rev. Alban Goodier.

There was something about this repetitive daily schedule and the method of preparing for prayer that has stayed with me over the years. Looking back now after thirty-two years, so much of the wisdom found in that content and method is still valid, even in the new and different context of religious life. The breadth and depth of this contemplative practice, focusing on the person of Jesus, can draw us inevitably toward a deeper relationship with him and a deeper commitment to life itself. Later on in my life as a Jesuit, as is true for most of us, I was involved in a number of very stressful and difficult work situations. One day I remember praying over the text of Jesus and the miraculous catch of fish. I had placed myself in the scene, and when we reached the moment to throw in the nets, Jesus was the first one to move to unravel them. I followed along with the others, and we began to unravel the nets. Jesus did not rush, and together we began to prepare the nets, layer after layer. Something inside of me began to unravel as well, and I felt able to enter into a dialogue with Jesus concerning certain parts of my life. I was able to see how all the different work elements were tangled up inside of me, but how important it was to take life one step at a time: step after step. The nets could not be untangled all at once, but had to be untangled slowly. I think by using this contemplative method much of my own emotion and feeling toward God was able to be released, and I was able to achieve some deep insights into my own life. During the rest of the day, I could feel the effects of this encounter. I felt as if a tube that had been clogged with mud and water had been cleaned out, and now the water was able to flow freely.

Much of my ministry work over the years has been involved with refugees and displaced people from El Salvador. I had visited that country many times over the years, before finally going to live and work there for three years with the Jesuit Refugee Service. One of the more traumatic experiences in my life, however, came when I was on a visit to El Salvador before going there to live.

Some of the workers from the Archdiocese of San Salvador had invited me to accompany them on a trip to bring supplies to some of the people who had been displaced because of the fighting that had been raging all around them due to the civil war. While driving down a country road, we suddenly found ourselves in what seemed to be the middle of a cross fire. After jumping out of the jeep and taking refuge in a local house, we were finally ordered out at gunpoint by the Salvadoran Army and arrested. The five of us were taken out of the area by helicopter and delivered to the headquarters of what was known as the "Treasury Police," an infamous branch of the Salvadoran security forces widely known for its mistreatment and torture of suspected "subversives."

When I was placed in the cell in the basement of that building, I remember very vividly undergoing an experience of what I can only call "connectedness." There was light falling into the room, and I knew it was afternoon. Somehow all of the different parts of my life seemed to come together, feeling more and more connected to each other as the time passed there in my cell. I could hear the screams of two young men being tortured not far away, with the constant flushing of water interspersed with their cries. Knowing the history of this place, I could only think of the hundreds of people who had suffered here, and I wondered if I would be just one more.

Nevertheless, I felt as if the years of trying to appropriate a method of contemplation had born fruit during those days in that basement cell. It was as if simultaneously I could both imagine and truly feel something of what Jesus experienced being jailed, knowing that his own death was near. I remember so vividly feeling a closeness to the Jesus who was persecuted and crucified. It was as if my own contemplation was suddenly turned on to "automatic pilot" and the power from this gave me strength to pass through the experience. In fact, the "connectedness," the experience of the present moment, the terror, the uncertainty, the finality — all blended in with the experience of Jesus. And this blending did not in any way lessen the actual suffering and fear I was feeling. But underneath it all, I felt a peace and, even as strange as it may sound, a happiness. This moment, in the midst of all the pain going on around and within me, is a unique and powerful memory.

So now, when I imagine and picture Jesus in specific Bible passages, I find that this is a method which has tremendous consequences for my life. By practicing this method of contemplation, placing our inner eye on Jesus, we are invited to share in a lifestyle that is governed by a conscious companionship with Jesus. Not only can we find a peace and be able to discern what to do, but in our daily life we begin to see and value things the way Jesus does. By using this method of contemplation over a number of years, we cannot help but relate more intensely to Jesus in a deepening intimacy.

It then seems we reach a point when the inner journey and the outer one seem to merge. We experience ourselves being deeply moved in prayer, contemplating the One who went before us, and we find ourselves meeting this same One in all sorts of ways during the day. Notwithstanding our ideal scenarios, where we are is not that important. What is paramount is that we put our eyes on Jesus, keeping our minds on him. When we do this, our inner and outer journeys do connect. Putting on the mind of Jesus doesn't exempt us from conflicts, problems, or the inconveniences that being committed to him entails.

But in holding to a contemplative heart, we find we can even embrace these things with a certain deep peace.

Daily we are told in a million ways what is going to make us happy. So we race around and try all different ways to love and be loved in order to be "happy." We tell ourselves, anticipating the next hurdle, "When I finish this, or when I gain this degree, or when I meet this person, or when I look like this... then I shall really be happy." Yet the answer Jesus offers us is a bit different. "The person who gives his or her life away, trying to live the Beatitudes, is the one who finds real happiness." Granted, this sounds simplistic.

But what if we recognized that it really is the Holy Spirit who is inviting us to use this method of contemplation? And what if we accepted this offer, and we actually found ourselves coming closer to Jesus? Wouldn't it be worth the risk? It is in his company that we can then experience what is of true value. It is with this experience that we find our inner and outer experiences coming together with a clarity and with a sense of his presence. It is possible to then taste the divinity of God in the very ordinariness and messiness of life's struggles. We can grasp more clearly that we are placed in certain circumstances, at certain moments, in order to contribute with Jesus in building up the Kingdom. This is what generates a deep happiness.

So what then does it mean to "deepen" our relationship with God? It means remembering events and moments which brought us somehow to feel a wonder at the One who seemed totally other and who comes very near to us: One who seemed to make us feel the value of living wonderfully beyond our means and expectations. We remember how these experiences absorbed us.

We remember these experiences as being somehow special. We want to experience them again and again so as to give them our full attention. In other words, we want to contemplate.

St. Ignatius of Loyola was very familiar with experiences like these. He was so absorbed in the life of Jesus that he wanted to pass on his experience to other people, not only other Jesuits. In his Spiritual Exercises, Ignatius devised a method of entering into the life of Jesus directly and intimately through the use of the imagination and senses. When praying through the life of Jesus, Ignatius didn't think it was enough just to "think" and "reflect" on Jesus' life. It was not enough to draw conclusions from the Gospel about how we should live. He thought we should move beyond the thinking process and "be there."

Ignatius divided his Exercises into four "weeks," each one roughly corresponding to a calendar week, but not necessarily identical to it. The first week is devoted more to "meditative" prayer, where we are indeed asked to "reflect" on, but also deeply feel, the reality of evil and sin, including our own. In the second through fourth weeks, we are asked to begin to "contemplate" the life of Jesus from Incarnation through the rest of his life, death, and resurrection. We don't start with considering certain theological truths and their possible applications in our lives. We are not engaged here primarily in the prayer of consideration. Rather we begin our prayer with a passage from Scripture and we try to imagine and feel what is taking place in the scene narrated.

Ignatius asks us to try to "apply" our senses as much as we can to what is happening in the scene. In doing this, we can find our hearts touched by the Spirit who chooses to reveal something of the "self" of God as the story proceeds. Thus does God invite us into a surprising experience of intimacy. From within this intimacy we can also be led to discern more easily what is right for us with regard to some decision to be taken. For example, I remember a person I was directing in a retreat who was trying to discern whether she should stay in a particular work placement. In her contemplations, it seemed that every time Jesus asked her to follow him, she couldn't do it. For some time she just stayed with this scene. She soon "discovered" (or saw more clearly) that God was not asking her to follow him the way she had first thought. Rather, she found that God had something different in mind for her, and it took her some time to grasp this. The ideal that she had thought out for herself and held on to was proving actually to be an obstacle. When she came once again to contemplate the call of Jesus, she felt herself being confirmed in her decision to leave that line of work.

What is paramount for Ignatius is our religious experience of God. Ignatius states that in the prayer of imaginative contemplation we become aware of the movement of different "spirits" within us. Are we moved to tears of consolation or are they tears of turmoil? When focusing with our heart on Jesus, do we find ourselves concerned and desiring to aid and to be a healing force for the sick and for the marginated? And does this movement of concern lead us toward God (consolation), or do we find ourselves inclined to run away, shying away from any type of commitment (desolation)?

What is primary is what "happens" in the contemplation itself. The passages of poetry in this book are meant to facilitate entering contemplatively into the Gospel scenes. They are meant to draw us into activating our inner senses, to notice inner details of inner events, and then to reflect on the inner movements of the "spirits" within us.

All Jesuits make the full thirty-day Spiritual Exercises of St. Ignatius at least twice in their lifetime: once at the beginning of their training and once again at the end of their formation period. Several years ago, I made my second thirty-day retreat at Gloucester, Massachusetts. This experience was somewhat different from my first long retreat eighteen years before. During this retreat, I would often sit by the stunning blue bay of Gloucester and just jot down some of the contemplations I had been praying about as a kind of journal entry. One day I read one of the contemplations on healing to another Jesuit. He told me the experience of hearing the passages moved him very much and asked for a copy of them. Other people have since made similar requests for these contemplations, and I have begun to see how they have been some help in forming a contemplative attitude in people.

A few years later, while directing Ignatian retreats in Wernersville, Pennsylvania, a person asked me, "Is all that is happening in my contemplation 'real'?" I think the answer to this question is very simple. The goal of authentic prayer is to take on the attitude and the mind of Jesus. While this answer may be "simple" and easy to say, we know that in practice it isn't easy at all, nor was it for Jesus' own friends. Looking at Jesus, attempting to be like him, requires a transformation and a changing within us.

But let us return to the retreatant's question about what is "real" in contemplation. I believe that as we develop and grow through life's events, simultaneously we progress correspondingly in our inner journey. In proportion as we contemplate, we find more and more that Jesus does keep us company and that we can converse with him as one does with a friend. What seems to happen is that attitudes and actions that once seemed foreign to us no longer seem so strange. In his own day Jesus challenged the powers around him. He entered the Temple, his Father's house, and not liking what he saw, he did not just speak the truth; he lived it and put it into action. Jesus, who was the contemplative par excellence, who loved going apart to be absorbed in his union with his Father, could easily integrate the driving out of the money changers of the Temple with his acts of compassion for all the needy. Indeed Jesus' own contemplative experience surely guided him in his outward expressions of word and action, setting the norm for all human living. And it is precisely as we join company through our contemplating with Jesus that we find our own hearts being invited by his peace to speak and act with the same faith and confidence. "By their deeds you shall know them."

I'd like to suggest a few ways in which this book can be used which are drawn from the fruit of my own and others' experience:

1. Find a comfortable and quiet place. Close your eyes, relax, leave concerns in God's care while you pray. Quietly remember that God is now with you and welcoming your full attention.

2. Slowly read the passage from the Gospel.

3. Allow yourself to become absorbed in what is taking place in the scene. How is each person feeling and what is each person doing? How am I feeling and what am I doing?

4. Now slowly read over the corresponding contemplation from this book. Use the contemplation like

a springboard to enter more deeply and completely into the scene.

5. Use your senses. Taste, touch, feel, smell, and see what is going on around you. Express yourself in the scene. Talk with those present. Become part of the scene itself.

6. Let God do the rest. Whatever thoughts, feelings and body sensations come, let them flow freely and allow them to deepen your contact with God. Often God reveals things to us that we could never have imagined or arrived at through merely "thinking" about them.

A final reflection: I know people who live and work in difficult places, doing humble and often dangerous work with the poor, and yet many of them do not profess any faith in God. But I believe some inner journey is taking place. In religious life as well, as time goes on, we become aware of the long haul of the inner journey. This journey cannot be "completed" in one or two years of intense work: there is a need for a constant contemplative dimension in our lives. At times we all pass through difficult phases in life, and we need the quality of our service to be nourished. This nourishment can only come from the support of loving friends, caring communities and families, and the experience of going deeper and deeper into the well of spirituality by means of both a disciplined and richly imaginative prayer.

baptism

matthew 3:13–17

At that time Jesus arrived from Galilee and came to John at the Jordan to be baptized by him. But John tried to prevent him, and said, "How is it you come to me: I should be baptized by you!"

But Jesus answered him, "Let it be like that for now. We must do justice to God's plan." John agreed.

As soon as he was baptized, Jesus came up from the water. At once, the Heavens opened to him and he saw the Spirit of God come down like a dove and rest upon him. At the same time a voice from heaven was heard, "This is my Son, the Beloved; he is my Chosen One."

i didn't want
to journey again
leave early
this terrain so familiar
sun lighting
darkened slopes
of the desert
walking slowly
along this path
leading me
to where the baptist was
walking along
this path
tears falling gently
wetting barren soil
what is happening
in my life?

it would be easier
to stay here
all these images
of late
images of so many
hungry children
of landless farmers
of tortured youth
looking ahead
not sure
really
where this path
was leading me
but i knew

i needed to continue
  walking
feeling myself walking
toward the jordan
how i missed many people
from my hometown
missed my routine
working with wood
feeling as if
i was being pushed
toward the images
  i carried within
approaching
where the baptist was
knew in this moment
looking at the crowds gathered
that it was my turn
to go under the water
maybe then i would know
people gathered
from all parts
i walked slowly
to the bank of the river
it seemed wider
than before
water seemed
  as if it was moving faster
  seemed as if it was deeper
  and bluer
i put my feet
into shallow water
looking at john
submerging these eager disciples

he was coming my way
his face stunned
jesus what are you doing here?
cousin
i have come
to be baptized
by you
john's face perplexed
jesus i would like to be baptized
by you
i had spoken enough
began to walk
    to a deeper part
    standing there
    feeling
how i was ready
john placing his hands
on my shoulder
slowly
guiding me deeper
i went deeper and deeper
now i was below
    the river's surface
could not see
    in the darkness
feel my days before
suddenly passing by
something new
feeling deep within
how i needed to surrender
    to surrender to my abba
    to begin. . . .
    to begin. . . .

in that moment
   underneath the water
   i saw clearly
the path . . .
i saw once again
all the images
   of people oppressed
but under this water
i saw the chain
   of oppression broken
i saw people free
a tremendous sensation
   filled my being
light again
hearing strongly
i will be with you
my son
you will not be alone
as you begin the work
of breaking chains
you will feel my love
everything after this water immersion
would be different
feeling same peace
as i felt below
in now knowing the path
my abba
was offering me
what had taken place
in the darkness
standing there
in the river
after so many days

since i left my hometown
i had been confused
not sure where you
   were calling me
under this water today
i tell you abba
i am ready
i am too tired
of seeing the heavy chains
placed around people
i tell you abba
i am ready
to work
so one day
this country will be a better place

call

matthew 4:18–20

As Jesus walked by the lake of Galilee, he saw two brothers, Simon called Peter, and Andrew his brother, casting a net into the lake, for they were fishermen. He said to them, "Come follow me, and I will make you fishers of people."

At once they left their nets and followed him.

i approached the shore
content with the catch
from last night
the satisfaction that comes
from pulling
in so many fish
during the night
felt good
seeing the size of the catch
and realizing
i would now be able
to buy
some more supplies
sliding
into shore
getting out of the boat
morning
breaking
behind the mountains
getting out
not knowing
what was going
to happen
spreading out nets
on the shore
thinking of my day ahead
when i saw a shadow
cross the nets
looking up
gazing
into the face of jesus

what was he doing here?
these hours are fisherman's
not a campesino's
from nazareth
standing up

jesus
good to see you
would you like some
of these fish?
we could prepare
a delicious breakfast
for you
you must be hungry
felt nervous inside
peter
was good you were successful
last night
i have another job
for you
peter
what would you think
of helping me?
the money is not too good
the hours are rather long
jesus
what would i think
of helping you?
to leave everything behind
and be a disciple
my head was spinning
didn't know
what to say

to follow you
jesus
i have watched
how you live
your invitation scares me
i am accustomed
to my routine
to my life
to follow you?
remembering back
to the dream i had
long ago
when i was young
a dream
in which
i dreamt
i saw a whole hillside
of lepers
faces covered
with sores
oozing with puss
hillside full with youth
hands chained from behind
cries of oppression
in the midst of them
one walked
healed the countless sick
liberated the enslaved
i never forgot that dream
as i look
into your face jesus
i see this one
from the dream

i feel an excitement
about the future
will i follow you?
i feel scared
but i remember
well the day
i had the dream
i ran behind this one
as he cured
as he freed
had a tremendous desire
to also work
like that
ever since
i had that dream
i have been in love
with that person
it is hard to explain
don't have
any words this morning
to explain it
will i follow you?
i remember
i ran behind this one
told him
about my neighborhood
what i experienced daily
the misery
the suffering
the hopelessness
he asked me
to learn from him
he asked me if

i wanted
to be a disciple
as i look at you jesus
i have the same feeling
as when i woke up
from that dream
i asked myself
what does it mean
to be in love with god?
how can i tell you
no jesus
i feel
i have all my life
been waiting
for you to ask me this

peter
it will be hard
there will be many
days and nights
when you will doubt
you have made
the right choice
it will just seem
too dark
but hold on
to your dream
never let it go
never lose
being in love
with god
let this love
free you to do great things

with this love
you too can
heal a hillside
full of sick
chained youth
come
let us begin
to let your dream
come true
follow me peter
let us begin
to share our lives
together

simplicity

matthew 12:1-8

It happened that Jesus walked through the wheat fields on a Sabbath. His disciples were hungry, and began to pick some heads of wheat and crush them to eat the grain. When the Pharisees noticed this, they said to Jesus, "Look at your disciples; they are doing what is prohibited on the Sabbath!"

Jesus answered, "Have you not read what David did when he and his men were hungry? He went into the house of God, and they ate the bread offered to God, although neither he nor his men had the right to eat it, but only the priests. And have you not read in the Law that on the Sabbath the priests in the Temple break the Sabbath rest, yet they are not guilty?

"I tell you, there is something greater than the Temple here. If you really knew the meaning of the words: *It is mercy I want, not sacrifice,* you would not have condemned the innocent.

"Besides the Son of Man is Lord of the Sabbath."

there had been so much rain
that the corn
grew high
sitting here this sabbath day
watching over
the cornfield
ever since i can remember
i had been forced to work
but this afternoon
i was enjoying
being outside of the city
away from the pressures
that i daily dealt with
pressures from so many directions
last night
arriving at this field
to begin my watch
i glanced up
at the stars
they were brilliant
sparkling
the moon was a sliver
i breathed out
and a heavy weight
was lifted off me
reflecting as i lay
in the middle of the cornfield
how do i ever get myself
in the middle
of such difficult situations?
my heart was sad

looking up
at the stars
realizing how i need
to slow down
not try to do everything
would try again
by being here
to see
what i could do differently
so my life
could reflect
the beauty of these fields
now the sun was out
another day
glancing in the distance
    watching
    a small group
make their way toward me
unusual for a sabbath
as i looked closer
saw it was the one
who healed
walking slowly with his friends
conversing
did not know
what to do
approach them?
or try to hide
among the corn stalks?
but i was tired
of hiding
always running from
any challenge

i wandered over
to where jesus was
with his friends
he had gathered some corn
into his hands
bending down

friends
my name is saul
i am in charge of these fields
may i sit
with you awhile?

jesus stood up
saul
come eat with us
as well
we have worked hard
have been under
much pressure
now it is time
to breathe in
the silence
the lushness
of this countryside
jesus
taking my hand
good to meet you saul
let us enjoy
the bright day
jesus began to talk about
yesterday
how when he was at the marketplace
and the pharisees challenged him

because he associated
with sinners
with lepers
with prostitutes
jesus spoke
of how he tried to explain
about the banquet table
where all are invited
but it was in vain
that is why
he was glad
they could be here
and remove themselves temporarily
from such conflicts
looking at jesus
this morning
listening to him
speak of how
life can get so complicated
moved me
to want to talk about
what i had been reflecting about
it always seemed
i had so much time to think
but never met
anyone like this
one in front
with whom to talk about it

jesus getting up
sensing my desire to talk
sitting next to me
handing me

a cup of cool water
jesus i have heard
many things about you
how you heal
so many with infirmities
jesus listening attentively
could sense
it mattered to him
what i said
it just seems
so much of the time
everyone only talks
about themselves
jesus
i have a neighbor
who was crippled
one day
i saw her
playing with her friends
she told me
someone named jesus
healed her
that is what i am asking of you
to cure me this morning
it is too hard
trying to make everything work
to be involved in
so many projects
being here with you
and your friends
i feel how much
i desire something simpler
feel i get pushed around

by so many demands
someone always wanting something
simpler
slower
jesus
yesterday before i came here
i ran around all day
with errands
for my family
my lessons for school
were never attended to
i felt pressure all day
yearning to be able to walk
instead of always running
jesus
in the middle of this cornfield
enjoying
this sabbath with you
i ask you
to help me
slow down
enjoy the beauties of nature
not try to do
so many things
may life
be less complicated
looking at jesus
knew
he understood so well
what i was speaking about
he reached over
and put his hands
which moments before were full

of corn
on top of my head
abba
i pray
for my brother saul here
i see that his heart
is good
but he is trying
to do everything
without relying more
on you
one creator
of wind and sun
let him learn
to walk
rather than run
let him
learn that nothing
is accomplished
by rushing
feeling the power from
jesus' hands
flow down
through my body
healing me
from so many moments
when i seemed lost
with pressures
feeling
jesus' fingers
strong
upon my head
as if

strong rays of light
flowing
down deeper and deeper
jesus
i feel
your hands
as you bring your healing
into my very depths
healing
from so many hurts
always seems i have
to make choices
between so many possibilities
thank you
for helping me
to see
how important
to enjoy the moment
know
it will never
be easy to know
what to choose
but i trust
that you will help me

as i was saying this
the two most disagreeable pharisees
with their friends
suddenly invaded
the intimacy of this moment
they gave us
glaring looks
with strong words

who are you all
to break the sabbath?
it is against our law
to travel
from where you came from
it is against our holy law
to gather corn
and crush it
on this holy day
are you not believers?
why do you
disregard our laws
so easily?

jesus
standing up
facing these pharisees
from the capital
you have come here
to condemn us
because
we enjoy the beauty
of this day
savoring the moment
eating the food
that nourishes us
like our ancestors did
your lives
are lived from the external
what people
will think of you
if you are legally
fulfilling a precept

we will continue
to be here
giving joy
to the one
who made all of this

the pharisees
reacted angrily
turning about
returning to their small worlds

jesus
thank you
for coming here today
i have learned
much from you
how to live

wedding

john 2:1-11

Three days later there was a wedding at Cana in Galilee and the mother of Jesus was there. Jesus was also invited to the wedding with his disciples. When all the wine provided for the celebration had been served and they had run out of wine, the mother of Jesus said to him, "They have no wine." Jesus replied, "Woman, your thoughts are not mine! My hour has not yet come."

However his mother said to the servants, "Do whatever he tells you."

Nearby were six stone water jars meant for the ritual washing as practiced by the Jews; each jar could hold twenty or thirty gallons. Jesus said to the servants, "Fill the jars with water." And they filled them to the brim. Then Jesus said, "Now draw some out and take it to the steward." So they did.

The steward tasted the water that had become wine, without knowing from where it had come; for only the servants who had drawn the water knew. So, he immediately called the bridegroom to tell him, "Everyone serves the best wine first and when people have drunk enough, he serves that which is ordinary. Instead you have kept the best wine until the end."

This miraculous sign was the first, and Jesus performed it at Cana in Galilee. In this way he let his Glory appear and his disciples believed in him.

i had been working
   preparing
   for the celebration
   of this wedding
   for weeks
my back ached
   from carrying these jars
   full of wine
   this celebration was beautiful
   i was enjoying
   the festivity
   because saul and ruth
   were very genuine
   authentic
   in their devotion
   to yahweh
i crept over to the courtyard
the rabbi had arrived
there was a seriousness
about the gathering
the parents stood to one side
ruth shone
the rabbi came close
to the couple
folded back her veil
will you love ruth
for the rest
of your life?
in good and hard times?
and ruth
will you love saul

for the rest
of your life?
in good and hard times?
to be close?
to be united?
i noticed
the cousin from nazareth
approach
the parents asking him
for a blessing
for their daughter
i came close
to hear his words

jesus began
abba one greater
i ask you
this afternoon
to bless
saul and ruth
in their union
you abba
have taught us
how you too
are the bridegroom
the lover of all your people
pursuing them
your love is without limits
let ruth and saul
also feel
this inexhaustible love
abba
may they spend

the rest of their days
dwelling
in this love

i looked
into jesus' eyes
they were filled
with tears
jesus
when you blessed this couple
when you talked
about yahweh as lover
i felt something jump
in my heart
to feel
this powerful
overflowing love of god
tell me more

friend david
at this very moment
god
is seeking your heart
as a desiring bridegroom
as a jealous lover
god is desiring
to also create this union
within you
if you let him
to be loved
to love
from the very depth
of your being

saying yes to this union
how short life is
how to be about
the most important thing
which is love
jesus sometimes
i feel what i see out there
is love
for one greater
when i walk home
in the evening
jesus
i feel this love
how
can i describe it to you?
i know
that it will never die
our bodies will decay
will turn to dust
but what it is to be loved
by yahweh
will never die
looking at jesus' face
lost in his gaze

david
bring me to the water pitchers
in the kitchen
i have been told
there is no more wine
we must celebrate
love today
going through the crowd

jesus
stopping
to speak to an elderly woman
to the ones working hard serving
jesus stopped
his language was universal
but
i watched him
carefully
as he slipped
through the crowd
  he was at home
  with the lowly
  the very well to do
  tried to grab
  hold of jesus
  but he always found
  himself with the poorest
  the divisions
  in this courtyard
  were dramatic
  jesus
  arriving with me
  to the kitchen
  even though
  there was tremendous commotion
i felt jesus
wanted to explain
more to me

david
can you still hear
the words

of love
between the bride and the groom
and how
   you spoke
of how your heart
   is sometimes moved
   by yahweh's love?
as you can see
   there is no more wine
   this water jar
   is empty
   there is a way
   of using this love
   you feel david
why do most people
seek what is comfortable
what is easy?
this love you feel
will lead to those
at the bottom
not where it is easy
you will feel
a love as strong
as when
you witnessed the love
between saul and ruth
even when
   you can't feel it
even when
   it is difficult
know that this love
for others
is connected

is one
with what you feel
when yahweh draws
   your heart
feel this love for yahweh
when your neighbor is dying
and you stay all night
as she goes to god
when you take a sick child
to see a doctor
when you confront the money changers
because
they have cheated a poor widow
it is the same love

jesus
putting his hands
into these jars
filled to the brim
with water

abba
   may we continue
   to celebrate your love
   with the most delicious wine yet
because this wine
will be celebrating
your love overflowing
for the brokenhearted
the sick
the oppressed
may this water
turn into delicious red wine
to celebrate

your love
for the poorest
david
don't forget
why you do what you do
i brought this wine
to the group
embarrassed to come forward
they were the most poorly dressed
i handed them
this red wine
their hands grateful
smiles covering their faces
   i never want to forget
   what jesus
   taught me this day
   how love is all
   love for each other
   love for yahweh
love for the least among us

freedom

luke 4:16-19

When Jesus came to Nazareth where he had been brought up, he entered the synagogue on the Sabbath as he usually did. He stood up to read and they handed him the book of the prophet Isaiah.

Jesus then unrolled the scroll and found the place where it is written: *The Spirit of the Lord is upon me. He has anointed me to bring good news to the poor, to proclaim liberty to captives and new sight to the blind; to free the oppressed and announce the Lord's year of mercy.*

jesus took the scroll
choosing to read
from isaiah
jesus lifting his voice
to all those
in this synagogue
whom he had known for years
the lord
has sent me
to bring good news to the poor
to set at liberty
those who are in prison
jesus reading these lines
powerful words
hanging in the air
jesus as he read
these lines
reflecting back
to the times
he had gone
to the prison
to visit
his friends from long ago
memories
of the condition
   and how
so many young
were thrown into the jail
by the romans
to rot away
faces of two friends

who had spent ten years
as they lived caged in
as animals
jesus' heart was moved
during those visits
when he watched
how the guards treated the prisoners
where was the compassion
in the hearts
of these guards?
jesus
remembered
as he read these words
strongly
of a good friend
who was wrongly convicted
of a crime he never committed
jesus
remembered seeing his
wife visit him
what anguish
spread across his wife's face
she spoke of the children
how hard it was to buy food
my friend would pound
his hand on the table
frustrated angry
at a system
that caged him in
for something he didn't do
why?
he would whisper
why?

the sadness that filled
ezekiel's eyes
oceans of sorrow
poured down his face
showing
what sprang from the hours
of being alone
thinking
of the ones he loved
jesus remembered
that afternoon
in the prison
he went over to ezekiel
sat down
next to him and his wife
jesus remembered
he wanted to say
so many things
but he couldn't find words
for the anguish
he felt
remembering
how he took their hands
and prayed with them
asking yahweh
to free him
from this confinement
that in the darkest moments
to reach out
for yahweh's hand
very close
and his wife?
jesus

remembered praying
that she not lose hope
as he prayed this
large tears
began to flow
down her face
saying so clearly
how hard
these years had been
separated
from the man
she loved
missing his presence
seeing their children
grow up
without their father
jesus
remembered telling judith
that he would visit
her at home
would bring something
for the children
maybe
bring them out
jesus
knowing that yahweh
was found
in visiting
these ones
who had been thrust
into this hopelessness
no doors open
no windows

no exit
only waiting
hoping against all odds

jesus
remembered
one time at the jail
seeing two young men
enter heads down
they had been sentenced
that day
and were given
the maximum of years
they couldn't talk
they just silently
buried their heads
in their hands
and you could hear
their cries of sadness

with all these memories
jesus
read so strongly
these lines from isaiah
feeling the great injustices
of the society
of the romans
of the high priests
the privileged classes
given everything
all the advantages
the best education
trips fine clothes
never found themselves

in the situations
to commit crimes
jesus remembered
in the jail
how many torturous stories
of children being abandoned
by their parents
being beaten
having fathers
who drank too much
not having enough
to eat
and one wonders
how they got to
these prisons
of the romans
it was so clear
that their lives
had been hard
from the start
jesus
remembering all these faces
of people
he visited
during this year
and he wondered
where yahweh was in all this
he just knew
that to be locked up
like this
lacking in hope
is where
one needed to be

to bring some hope
  some light
  some good news
that god
had not forgotten them
there is a silence
here
filling the spirit
filling

fear

matthew 14:22–33

Immediately Jesus made his disciples get into the boat and go ahead of him to the other side, while he sent the crowd away.

And having sent the people away, he went up the mountain by himself to pray. At nightfall, he was there alone. Meanwhile, the boat was very far from land, dangerously rocked by the waves for the wind was against it.

At daybreak, Jesus came to them walking on the lake. When they saw him walking on the sea, they were terrified, thinking that it was a ghost. And they cried out in fear. But at once Jesus said to them, "Courage! Don't be afraid. It's me!" Peter answered, "Lord, if it is you, command me to come to you walking on the water."

Jesus said to him, "Come." And Peter got out of the boat, walking on the water to go to Jesus. But, in face of the strong wind, he was afraid and began to sink. So he cried out, "Lord, save me!" Jesus immediately stretched out his hand and took hold of him, saying, "Man of little faith, why did you doubt?"

As they got into the boat, the wind dropped. Then those in the boat bowed down before Jesus saying, "Truly, you are the Son of God!"

jesus had remained alone
to pray
we would catch up
with him tomorrow
all night long
we had done battle
against the wind
struggling hard
to get to the other shore
had been hard days
ready to reach shore
suddenly
a bright form
could be seen
in the distance
fear spreading through the boat
shape approaching
seeing it is jesus
jesus saying
do not be afraid
it is i
if it is you jesus
let me come to you
i have been blown about
all night in this boat
i desire
to come closer to you
my life does not make sense
without you
jesus
saying

come here peter
so i slowly
put my hands
on the sides
of the boat
lifting myself out
of the boat
felt good to be freed
from such narrow confines
putting
one foot in front of the next
walking on water
looking at your
face jesus
right into your eyes
watching your smile
lighting up
your face
lost in your gaze
feeling i can do anything
feeling a confidence
flowing from you jesus
when jesus
have i trusted you
so much
to leave my security?
and try to do
great things
with risks?
with dangers?
how long was i lost
in jesus' gaze
jesus

i need to step
out of the boat
daily
and as importantly
need to really
focus my looking
at you
as you give me
the strength
to walk on this lake
as i gaze
into your face
i tell you jesus
you are beautiful
to behold
you are the one
that i love
need to keep
my eyes on you
jesus
why haven't i walked
on water before?
because i have not kept
my eyes on you
feeling a strong gust
of wind
push me forward
thinking
i can't
in no way
actually be walking
on water
it's impossible

can never happen
all these doubts
began to pull me
into dark waters
as this happened
when i took my eyes
away from jesus
now i began to sink
quickly
all these doubts
about everything
doubts about our work
was it doing any good?
doubts if it was worth it
to leave my family?
doubts if we would really
achieve anything
as if tremendous weights
began to pull me
downward
slowly slipping into
cold water
seemed everything
was finished
when i could barely
catch a glimpse
of jesus
from surface of water
totally immersed
with all the strength
of my being
i yelled
jesus please

help me
i'm drowning
i'm drowning
from all this water
jesus help me
i prayed this
with all my being
jesus help me
these words strong
shot out
into the dark
echoing across the surface
stronger
more forceful than raging wind
more passionate
than breaking white crested waves
jesus help me
filling the night air
jesus help me
shaking the darkness
of the early morning
as if
i repeated these words
a thousand times
again and again
coming across the lake
jesus help me
why did i take
my eyes from you?
why do i always do this?
jesus help me
feeling
the two most comforting hands

put themselves around
my shoulders
feeling jesus' presence
as he reached
under my arms
lifted my shaking self
jesus knew
how scared i was
felt safe
in his embrace
out of raging water
jesus
holding me tight
why
jesus did i take my eyes
off you?
peter
why do you
have so many doubts?
why do you
try to be
so self-reliant
depending
on your own power
feel me close
to you now
draw strength
from me
there is
no other way
otherwise
you will be always
drowning in the water

jesus
lifting me back
into the boat
wind calming
feeling inside
how grateful
jesus
how you saved me
from dark waters
help me always
to keep my eyes
on you

matthew

mark 2:13–17

When Jesus went out again beside the lake, a crowd came to him and he taught them. As he walked along, he saw a tax collector sitting in his office. This was Levi, the son of Alpheus. Jesus said to him, "Follow me." And Levi got up and followed him.

And it so happened that while Jesus was eating in Levi's house, tax collectors and sinners were sitting with him and his disciples for there were indeed many of them. But there were also teachers of the Law of the Pharisees' party, among those who followed Jesus, and when they saw him eating with sinners and tax collectors, they said to his disciples, "Why! He eats with tax collectors and sinners!"

Jesus heard them and answered, "Healthy people don't need a doctor, but sick people do. I did not come to call the righteous but sinners."

early in the afternoon
   was the time
   that so many pilgrims
   entered the city
   sitting at my desk
   my two assistants
   were busy
   stopping pilgrims
   forcing them to pay taxes
   that were demanded
i had slipped
nearby
observing the throngs
of people paying the little they had
looking at faces
of matthew's assistants
the greed exuding from every pore
matthew looked distracted
far away
dreaming about something
dreaming that life
could be different
i came close to his table
he looked up at me
was surprised to see me
jesus
you don't have to pay anything
you have nothing to declare
matthew
i came here
to speak with you

come over here
we left the crowds
we sat down
looking across the land
all the way to jerusalem
the sun was hot
so matthew
how have you been?
what were you thinking
as you collected
that money?
was your heart into it?
i could tell this question
broke strongly into matthew
he became very serious
    intense
starting to cry
silently
jesus
how did i ever get involved
in this type of work?
i never
thought it would do this
    to me
the emptiness
the self-hate
i am rejected
by my community
looked upon
as a traitor
sure i have a beautiful house
have fancy possessions
but what does all this matter

in comparison
to being at peace with yourself?
   being at peace with yourself
jesus
i desire this
more than what you imagine
   at peace with myself
so i can sleep at night
now i wake up
i wonder
what i have become
thinking before
riches
could make me happy
never
you cannot buy
peace of heart
how i would trade
anything
for that peace
matthew
what do you think
   about helping me
   with my work?
jesus
helping you?
my world froze
nothing moved
help you?
but everyone calls me
   a sinner
   an undesirable
matthew

stop
i see something in you
that no one else does
i see who you really are
and that you desire
to do greater things
are generous
you made a mistake
but don't let that
ruin your whole life
jesus
in this moment
i feel
i really can change
looking at you jesus
i feel strongly
   you accept me
   the way i am
   it is from this love
   i feel the strength
   to change
that i don't have
to spend the rest of my life
doing this unjust work
taking coins
from my pocket
tossing them into the valley
jesus
i want to be free
not to be attached
to all this travesty
i never regretted that gesture
jesus

i thank you
for inviting me
to change my work
and learn from you
what it is
to be a disciple
thank you
for accepting me enough
to know i can change

healing

luke 4:40 – 41

At sunset, people suffering from many kinds of sickness were brought to Jesus. Laying his hands on each one, he healed them. Demons were driven out, howling as they departed from their victims, "You are the son of God!" He rebuked them and would not allow them to speak, for they knew he was the Messiah.

light of the day falling
shadows seen from the trees
smells from the lake
waiting
all day outside
of peter's house
all day
wanting to go
by the water
before i met
the master from nazareth
so i escaped
from the crowd
turned right
from peter's house
soon at the shore of the lake
rays of sun falling
dancing
across the surface
glanced and saw jesus
he was standing there
staring out
at first i wanted to go
back quickly
but something moved me
to go and approach him
jesus felt my presence
and he turned around
i came closer
jesus good to meet you
my name is jonathan

jesus speaking of the sparkling
on the water
sitting down with him
watching
the sun slowly disappear
jesus began to speak
about how he was moved
by so many ill
outside of peter's house
he said he had been here
in capernaum for a week
saw one of his feet scarred
he acted
as if he had known me
all my life
jonathan
you see that gleaming
across the lake
yes jesus
is beautiful to watch
there is power in healing
jesus was silent
i really don't desire
that these marginated folks
have to endure
such suffering
on many levels
his hands reached down
and grabbed a handful of sand
he closed his eyes
to be whole
to be healed
jonathan

could you help me
this afternoon to heal
to lay hands on to heal?
i stared at jesus
had not told him
anything about myself
what could i say?
of course i will help you
powerful strong like the sun
jesus reaching over
laying his hands on my head
i closed my eyes
i felt the heat
from the sun burning
not even mentioned
to jesus
why i had come
this was not important anymore
felt his healing
flow through my body
not one word at first
from jesus
just feeling
like sun burning
flowing into my body
warming
going to my very depth
feeling how
the sparkles within
glittering
down deeper and deeper
to where
the very center is

prayer

luke 11:1–8

One day Jesus was praying in a certain place and when he had finished, one of his disciples said to him, "Lord, teach us to pray, just as John taught his disciples." And Jesus said to them, "When you pray, say this:

Father, hallowed be your name,
may your kingdom come,
give us each day the kind of bread we need,
and forgive us our sins, for we also forgive all who
     do us wrong,
and do not let us fall in temptation."

Jesus said to them, "Suppose one of you has a friend and goes to his house in the middle of the night and says: 'Friend, lend me three loaves, for a friend of mine who is traveling has just arrived and I have nothing to offer him.' Maybe your friend will answer from inside: 'Don't bother me now; the door is locked and my children and I are in bed, so I can't get up and give you anything.' But I tell you, even though he will not get up and attend to him because he is a friend, yet he will get up because the other is a bother to him, and he will give him all he needs."

it was early in the morning
   nothing was moving yet
   in the village
   only sounds of dogs
   barking in the distance
stars still studded the sky
jesus needing to be alone
to pray to his abba
i left where i was sleeping
   and followed jesus
   to the water
   slowly walking along the path
   coming to the shore
   a stillness in these morning hours
   watching jesus
   as he sat
   and began to converse
   knew
   i was involved in sacred space

left
where i was
   and went
   and sat next to jesus
   hearing softly

abba
i come here this morning
could not sleep very well
i feel you close to me
this morning
it is good to be here

all night long
images of the people
i had dealt
with during the day
floated in me
i was restless
sometimes
i feel so powerless
abba
just being with you here
feeling your presence
fills me with a peace
   a tranquility
need your help
having been so overwhelmed
by the forces of oppression
always looming before us
need your help
it seems as if everyone
thinks they know
who you are
as if they own you
rattling off some words
and their hearts, abba?
i feel
when i am with you
that you set my heart
on fire
a happiness permeates
within so strongly
that i feel how much
you love me
you love me abba

honestly sometimes
i don't understand
why you sent me here
it all seems so hard
abba
i tell you this morning
   i am trying
   my very best
   to do your will
   sometimes
   it seems like
   all is a failure
   is dark
   is empty
as we get stepped
on by the powerful
abba
i feel your love
this keeps me trying
all these friends
folks from the village
ask me
how to pray
how to be
with you
abba
to me
it would be like asking
how are you supposed
to be
with the people
you love
it's so essential

to be with you
in this silence
listening
beyond the stillness
to your voice
sharing
what is in the heart
and in doing this
able to see
have more vision
where i am going
what you desire
sitting here this morning
i also feel
how you are pleased
that i try
to live
what i receive
from you
sitting here this morning abba
i ask you
do you want me
to go to jerusalem?
sometimes
i feel so strongly
that is what you desire
other times
i feel i should go back
to capernaum
and teach the disciples more
abba
sometimes
they just don't understand at all

so abba
i desire to be guided
by you
that you
be part of that decision
listening in the silence
as the water rolled into shore
if i go to jerusalem
this would bring matters
to a head
challenging the power structures
is this your will?
horizon reddening with morning light
deep colors
intensified by heat
barrenness of the desert mountains
abba
last night i could not sleep
all night long
i thought and thought
about this decision
looking out at this water
feeling
as if a soft breeze
blowing within
letting me see
that you do desire
abba
that i go to jerusalem
and i feel
so strongly
that no matter
what happens

abba
you will be with me
your presence
   sun appearing
above the mountains
jesus turning around

jesus
i watched as you prayed
i ask you
to teach me
to pray like you do

peter
look at what
we saw
when we went
to the temple yesterday
the loud voices
repeating
psalm after psalm
the demanding of certain needs
so peter
you ask me
how you speak
with the one
whom you love
for me
i need to be
with my abba
in order
to keep the vision
of how
to do his will

we do not need
to say so many words
but
to be in our abba's presence
listening
to what he desires
for us
very simple

nicodemus

john 3:1–10

Among the Pharisees there was a ruler of the Jews named Nicodemus. He came to Jesus at night and said, "Rabbi, we know that you have come from God to teach us, for no one can perform miraculous signs like yours unless God is with him."

Jesus replied, "Truly, I say to you, no one can see the kingdom of God unless he is born again from above."

Nicodemus said, "How can there be rebirth for a grown man? Who could go back to his mother's womb and be born again?" Jesus replied, "Truly, I say to you: Unless one is born again of water and the Spirit, he cannot enter the kingdom of God. What is born of the flesh is flesh, and what is born of the Spirit is spirit. Because of this, don't be surprised when I say: 'You must be born again from above.'

"The wind blows where it pleases and you hear its sound, but you don't know where it comes from or where it is going. It is like that with everyone who is born of the Spirit."

Nicodemus asked again, "How could this be?" And Jesus answered, "You are a teacher in Israel, and you don't know these things!"

it was dark
i knew what i was going to do
was dangerous
but inside i had this strong desire
to meet this teacher
so many had spent time
condemning him at our meeting today
i knocked on the door
sounds echoing against the walls inside
used to knocking at fancy doors
but not at doors like this one
a young girl arriving
looking shocked seeing my fine robes
my chains of gold around the neck
felt judged by her
thinking maybe it would be better
to go back to my side of town
did not know
what to say
suddenly i blurted out
i would like to speak
with jesus
what was i saying
here i was
looked upon as the enemy
asking to see
the one we had given
all the problems to
two worlds meeting at that door
in the darkness
world of privilege position wealth

and world of simplicity
struggling to survive
she had on a brown garment
clean neat patched
wondering how could
there be such
a screeching chasm
between her world and mine
my parents leaders
of the synagogue were able to send me
to the best schools
had a large house
all the comforts i desired
yet
looking at this young one
answering the door
felt empty inside
as if i did not know anything
as if i really did not know god
sure i knew so many passages
by memory
all of a sudden
standing in front of this open door
asking to see jesus

everything became clearer
all the parts of the picture
began to be rearranged
yearning to know
really know god
a deep desire sprang up
within my heart
felt as if i were falling down

from the highest part of jerusalem
what is your name
feeling bad
i have never asked the servants
in my house their names
she smiled my name is sarah
i asked to meet jesus
am looking for this teacher
even before i met him
my world is being turned
upside down
i'll get him
she uttered
   come in and wait
grateful for the invitation
feeling dizzy
what is happening to me?
why am i feeling like this?
came out of mere curiosity
but this whirlwind experience
was so unexpected

looking up
peering into a face
hearing the words
my name is jesus
jesus
echoing within me
i stammered
my name is nicodemus
i would like to speak
with you
we passed by many groups

of campesinos from the province
coming to this city
for the high holy days
sitting sharing food
talking quietly
in the cover of the night
we sat at the end
of the property
overlooking the whole city
fires burning
lighting up the darkness
jesus
i have felt
i have wanted to meet you
for a long time
everyone is talking about you
i knocked on this door
asking to see you
all of a sudden
my world got out of focus
nicodemus
it is good
you no longer feel safe
on old ground
your world is cracking apart
because it was built
on the sweat
of poor people
like the ones gathered here
you need to start over
be born again
looking into jesus' face
noticing his torn robe

the thickness of his beard
the cuts on his hands
as if he too
had been working in the fields
jesus how do i do that?
i am an important leader
i have so many under me
that depend on me
nicodemus
look again behind you
i turned
and saw weathered worn women
  cooking over blazing fires
  children running quickly
  bent over old men
  crippled from too much work
  under burning sun
look closely
i'll count to three
one two three
again it happened
seeing more than what was there
or perhaps it was always there
but i never saw it
  never understood it
  do i want to be born again?
  i felt myself
  taking off my fine linen
  my gold
  putting on a tan robe
  walking over
  to the group
  sitting around the circle

handing them these goods
sitting in the circle
jesus
joining us
whoever wants to be born again
to be one
with your brothers and sisters
not superior
not more important
but brother
that is what you are feeling
right now
your arrogant world is falling apart
you are feeling
the connections
that exist
between all people
not just with the people
from your pharisee-like class
felt good
to be sitting
in this circle
how could i ever go back
to the world
where i lived
before i was born again?
thank you jesus
for letting me feel this connection

two by two

mark 6:6-12

Jesus then went around the villages teaching. He called the Twelve to him and began to send them out two by two, giving them authority over evil spirits. And he ordered them to take nothing for the journey except a staff; no food, no bag, no money in their belts. They were to wear sandals and were not to take an extra tunic.

And he added, "In whatever house you are welcomed, stay there until you leave the place. If any place doesn't receive you and the people refuse to listen to you, leave after shaking the dust off your feet. It will be a testimony against them."

So they set out to proclaim that this was the time to repent. They drove out many demons and healed many sick people by anointing them.

jesus we have been with you
   for a year
   have watched
as you have cured people
have spoken to the crowds
have walked many miles
with you
this morning you ask us
   to go in twos to different parts
what are we supposed
to do jesus?
what are we supposed
to say jesus?
would prefer to stay with you
it seems challenging
to go to that town
by the lake of galilee
what are we going to find?
how do i talk
about
this kingdom of god
   jesus placing his hands
   on top of my head
   feeling presence
   flow into me

feeling this very same power
flowing
as i walked
feeling i knew
what i was to do
along with my companion jonathan

arriving at evening time
the sun was falling
behind the hills
children running
through dusty streets
seeing friends i knew
saw the woman named sara
who lived across the street
she hobbled horribly
because of fever

all around us
were folks
bent over from suffering
knew in that moment
why jesus had blessed us
asked us to prepare the way
for him
because he did not desire
to see his people suffer
put my hands
on sara
asking yahweh to heal her

well into the evening
jonathan and myself
prayed over the sick
the power the connection
it made with the people
was powerful
as we walked down
to the shore
of the lake
knew things

would be different now
could feel a deep healing
that had taken place

evening
looking at all the youth
return from fishing
saw some so lost
how do you let
them feel this power of jesus?
inviting them
to sit around with us
asking them about themselves
about the problems
of the village
an enthusiasm flowing rapidly
much energy
asking them
if they would like to meet
the master from nazareth
enthused about the idea
to meet the one
whom so many were talking about

that night
at the shore of the lake
looking out at the ripples
across the dark mass of water
the moon's reflection brilliant
feeling in my heart
how i would like
the ones i had spoken
with in the afternoon
to know jesus

to talk with him
i knew
their lives would be different
with this contact
with the one
who had changed our lives
so much
remembering the stories
i had heard
from so many
the exploitation by the romans
the kidnapings
the repression against anyone
protesting the heavy taxes
hardly enough to eat
because of the exploitation
one young miriam told
of her brother abel
who was in jail
in the garrison nearby
the conditions so cruel
looking out at the water
feeling the water
lap against my feet
again and again
thinking
how my life
   had been changed
   by knowing the master
   how i saw
   everything so differently
   was here
   in his name

desired deeply this night
that
this pueblo
also know the one
who had changed my life
could not leave this spot
letting this desire
be connected to the stillness
of the night
it was almost painful
how much i was feeling all this
that life
would be different
if somehow
they knew
that life
could truly be hopeful
for them
and just as the sick
  were healed
  in the morning
  the pain
  the infirmities
were taken away
  in his name
so likewise they would
be different
by knowing jesus
sitting there
all during the night
a few signs of dawn
appearing in the distance
turning to my right

seeing jesus close by
my heart leapt

asking me
if i had prepared the way for him
could not think
didn't know what to say
jesus
all night i have been here
staring out at the water
would like you
to meet the people
i have been with
life is so hard for them
looking into jesus' face
saw in his expression
how much he also desired this
everything stopped
   feeling how much
   jesus
   was grateful
for what we had done
   in this pueblo
for our desire
for the people
to know him
how important
to know you
to see how you move us
to change this slavery
to be liberated
from so much oppression
soon others from the town

joining us
jesus speaking about his abba
about how he desires us
to be whole
not to have to suffer
under such conditions
glad i could prepare
   the way
as i watched
the faces of the people
change
spending the day
with this one
knew that
what i was feeling
in my heart
was love strong
flowing in me
around me
didn't understand it
but knew
that the group
was also feeling
this
same experience
that i had in my heart
when
i heard scriptures
read in the synagogue
how yahweh
rescued his people
from slavery
how he sent

holy men and women
to be with his people
this afternoon
taking in this encounter
knew
i felt this same love
flowing from this teacher
powerful

well

john 4:5-14

He came to a Samaritan town called Sychar, near the land that Jacob had given to his son Joseph. Jacob's well is there. Tired from his journey, Jesus sat down by the well; it was about noon. Now a Samaritan woman came to draw water and Jesus said to her, "Give me a drink." His disciples had just gone into town to buy some food.

The Samaritan woman said to him, "How is it that you, a Jew, ask me, a Samaritan and a woman, for a drink?" (For Jews, in fact, have no dealings with Samaritans.) Jesus replied, "If you only knew the Gift of God! If you knew who it is that asks you for a drink, you yourself would have asked me and I would have given you living water.... Whoever drinks of this water will be thirsty again; but whoever drinks of the water that I shall give will never be thirsty; for the water that I shall give will become in him a spring of water welling up to eternal life."

everyone desiring to go
into the pueblo
needed some time
  to be alone
away from the crowds
sitting in the shade
breathing out
all the pressures
  the demands of past days
listening
to the silence
of the desert
sounds of animals
in the distance
watching the heat
rise from the sand
would be good
to rest here
  for an hour
  before we continue
  we could eat
  here in the coolness
reflecting back
on all the people
we had talked with yesterday
the demands
remembering
especially
one youth who was paralyzed
i had talked with him
last year

i felt connected
to him
he talked about his accident
could feel tears
up in my eyes
remembering jonathan

sitting in the silence
of the desert
i ask you abba
to remember him
when he was cured
his face changed
his happiness spread
across his face
a desire strong
filling my heart
that jonathan can know you
abba
whirlwind in front
sweeping up dry weeds
to know you
to experience you
in this moment
a shadow crossing the well
a surprised look
on the woman's face
thinking how
i can have some
of the water deep
within this well
my name is jesus
what is yours?

rebecca
astonishment
crossed her face
what are you talking about
i'm not of your religion
you should not be talking to me
i'm just telling you
i'm very thirsty
and need a drink of water
you need to let
your bucket sink down
very deep
and to experience
something more
to touch the divine
to know
the one who made this world
to go down deeper
once you experience this water
at your depths
you will never be thirsty again
never
i'm not following you
uttered this confused one
sitting down
next to me
placing her bucket
on top of the well
i came here this morning
because i can no longer
come at regular hours
without people
laughing at me

for being so confused
in love
i just seem to get into trouble
with my heart
i have been used by some
i took
the bucket throwing it
down deep into
the well
down deeper and deeper
rebecca felt something happening
within her
as the bucket
fell down deeper and deeper
it was like
this was happening
within her
to go through layers
of alienation hurt confusion
resting at the bottom of the well
where there was peace
to know god
to experience god
what did you do
to have this happen?
i perceive
you are a prophet
a holy person
to create
such a religious experience
within
i realize
how my life

has been so empty
i have been so thirsty
for what you have offered me
it is as if all my life
i have been searching
for the bucket
to move beyond the surface
to the depths
all the things
that have meant so much to me
now seem meaningless
jesus
help me
not to lose
what i am feeling
help me to be grounded
in this presence strong
an experience
that is connected
to you jesus
and who you are
what you are about
offering rebecca
the water
bringing it to her lips
drinking slowly
refreshing water

jesus
again i feel
a presence flow through me
connected to love
desiring jesus

in this moment
to be close to god
reflecting on
how i was
always agitated
looking outside
for what
can only be found
within
jesus

deep loss

luke 7:11-17

A little later Jesus went to a town called Naim and many of his disciples went with him — a great number of people. As he reached the gate of the town, a dead man was being carried out. He was the only son of his mother and she was a widow; there followed a large crowd of townspeople.

On seeing her, the Lord had pity on her and said, "Don't cry." Then he came up and touched the stretcher and the men who carried it stopped. Jesus then said, "Young man, awake, I tell you." And the dead man got up and began to speak, and Jesus gave him to his mother. A holy fear came over them all and they praised God saying, "A great prophet has appeared among us; God has visited his people." And throughout Judea and the surrounding country, people talked about Jesus' deeds.

it was hot
sweat was pouring down my face
it was heavy carrying this litter
with david
but not as heavy
   as the sorrow of his mother ruth
   he was her hope
   after her husband was killed
   by the romans
   david had worked the fields
and barely made enough
for the both of them
what would she do now?
i had gone to school with david
he was bright
hard working
if we only had
had enough money
we could have brought him
to the doctor
but what good
would that have done
if there was no money
to pay for the medicine?
so david had an agonizing death
not wanting to leave his mother
alone
so much work to be done
losing a husband and a son
in one year
certainly the weight of this litter

the pressure against the shoulders
was nothing in comparison
to the sorrow wide
   pounding
   within the heart of ruth
   heavy
leaving large gates
of the city
to put in the ground
david's body
we had prepared him
for the burial
as we were leaving
the confines of the city
i looked
in the distance
and caught sight
of the one they call jesus
he was traveling
with a group of friends
   nearing the litter
   jesus stopping
   taking in the situation
looking into the face of ruth
i had seen jesus
conversing long hours
with david
this death has caught him
by surprise
jesus moved
by the grief
flowing
from the heart

of ruth
we stop
jesus comes over
and embraces ruth
expressing his sorrow
jesus
knows what this loss
will mean to her
he thinks
of his own mother mary
how hard it was for her
a widow
jesus felt connected
to this trembling woman
jesus knelt down
next to the litter
he took david's hand
rubbing it
talking to him
feeling compassion deep
from jesus
touching this dead one
i wanted to tell jesus
he shouldn't do this
it was going
to make him impure
but the gentleness
the tenderness
in which jesus
   stroked david
   touched me
   no one moving
   all concentrating

on the love
jesus had for david
and his mother
jesus taking his hand
rubbing it against
david's cold forehead
the finality of death
passing his hands
over his eyes
shut to all light
now focused in
on the other world
jesus
did not hurry
taking all the pain
into himself
i looked at his face
he wanted so much
to bring life
i bent down next to him
jesus buried his face
in david's chest
praying quietly softly
abba this afternoon
i bring before you
our brother david
may you let your spirit
be in him again
how much
his mother
needs him
how much he has before him
abba

i hear nothing
in his chest
no heart beat
no sign of life
i ask you to bring forth
spirit
life
to beat again
slowly the chest
of david
began to move
heart beating
spirit
jesus helping him
sit up
talking with him
what had happened?
asking for some water
washing his face
handing him something to eat
huge smile of gratitude
passing over david's face
helping david up
jesus bringing him
over to where ruth stood
son embracing mother
jesus left the group
happy to bring life
into this group
life

storm

luke 8:22–25

One day Jesus got into a boat with his disciples and said to them, "Let us go across to the other side of the lake." So they set out, and as they sailed he fell asleep. Suddenly a storm came down on the lake and the boat began to fill with water, and they were in danger. The disciples then went to Jesus to wake him, saying, "Master! Master! We are sinking!" Jesus woke up. He rebuked the wind and the rolling waves; the storm subsided, and all was quiet.

Then Jesus said to them, "Where is your faith?" They were afraid; they were astonished as well and said to one another, "Who can this be? See, he commands even the wind and the sea and they obey him."

we had been with jesus
many months now
life passed so quickly
i had never prayed
for healing
until i met jesus
for hours
i have watched
as he laid hands
and cured lepers paralytics
the old and the young
   it was now evening time
   we had been speaking
   with the crowds
for days and days
no end to the needs
no limit to the demands
of this suffering people
last night
   we were so exhausted
   could not sleep
   nothing
we needed to escape
   needed to get some distance
   jesus asking us
   to get the boats ready
   sun falling behind the mountains
   we hurried down to the shore
climbing aboard
large wooden carefully crafted vehicle
we pushed

out from shore
first signs of night
as stars appeared above
soon we were moving
  across the water
  rapidly
at last
we could breathe
jesus
taking off his sandals
large cut
across his foot
removing outer garment
using it
as a pillow
putting it behind his head
staring up at the heavens
sitting next to jesus
the wind blowing strongly
against jesus' exhausted face
as if almost
a storm was approaching
that would be our luck
soon my head
was nodding
i was fast asleep
being awakened
by the violent
rocking of the boat
in one instant
could tell
what was happening
now no longer

clear bright heavens
rather dark black clouds
wind stronger
and stronger
this had never happened
to me before
all of a sudden
this violent storm
pushed over
into the boat
a large raging wave
thoughts of yesterday
faces of the children
who were sick
and jesus touched
brought to himself
healed
then another large wave
swept into the boat
this time i had images
of the long meetings
we had with the disciples
endless
fear had begun
to enter my being
as another more forceful wave
broke into the boat
strong
conversations filled my mind
of the arguments
with the pharisees
more and more white
could be seen

across the lake's surface
  a storm
  blowing in
  wave after wave
  memory after memory
  of hard experiences
  overwhelming
  as we began to go under
frantically
using our large containers
to bail
out the water
never expected this storm
feeling in this moment
crushed by the storm
by the pace
of recent months

it was all too much
wave after wave
wave after wave
glancing
at where jesus lay
how could he stay asleep?
we are going to drown
approaching jesus
shaking him awake
jesus opening his eyes
sitting up
jesus
we have been struck
by a sudden storm
violent

jesus keep us
from drowning
jesus taking my hand
we only create storms
inside
when we take on
too much
too many waves
will sink this boat
and the one next to us

jesus
how are we supposed
to change this?
all these waves
create a storm violent
filling ourselves
with too much water
it gets to a point
where there is no turning back
the boat will sink
it is good
this is not the case
there is still time peter
to be rescued
from the force
of raging waves
freed by overpowering storm
peter from now on
we will prevent
so many waves
from entering
jesus

reaching into the water
throwing it into the air
now less water in the boat
jesus
reaching in again
and hurling into the darkness
another wave
again less water
   as jesus
   did this
   three more times
   the storm dissipated
   the atmosphere
was more focused
felt grateful in my heart
knew jesus was showing me
how to be focused
to do less
so drowning waves
cannot enter
so unexpectedly
now a calm peaceful lake
no more white caps
no more waves
crashing into the boat
jesus
help me
the next time
i begin
to let waves
crash over into the boat
help me
not to enter

into this stormlike state
but rather help me
to see
as you do
what to do
each moment
jesus
you never seem
to be drowning
spirit
strong
seems to empower you
to choose wisely
not letting in
too much water

martha

luke 10:38 – 42

As Jesus and his disciples were on their way, he entered a village and a woman called Martha welcomed him to her house. She had a sister named Mary who sat down at the Lord's feet to listen to his words. Martha, meanwhile, was busy with all the serving and finally she said: "Lord, don't you care that my sister has left me to do all the serving?"

But the Lord answered, "Martha, Martha, you worry and are troubled about many things, whereas only one thing is needed. Mary has chosen the better part, and it will not be taken away from her."

there were four rooms left
since morning i had been
cleaning
working
to get everything ready
four rooms left
always piled documents
accumulated work
and more
four o'clock
a knock
at the door
walking from room to
the entrance whitewashed
passing by piled-up documents
feeling a heaviness
the knock from the door
echoing
i'm coming
i'm coming
my brother should be home
soon
wondering where mary was
noticing
as i rushed toward the door
all the areas
that needed to be cleaned
the dirt from this street
is too much
finally arriving at the door
opening slowly the latch

swinging open
jesus
with his friends
my brother joining them
jesus
good you stopped by
you all look hot
you look hungry
a million thoughts
raced through my mind
how can i get
enough food ready
in time for the meal
mary arriving
mary
we need to get going
jesus
passing through the door
mary
stood there watching
this group
gather quietly
into our large gathering place
i told martha
i would get them some water
some towels
soon this room
was filled
with the music
of friends interconnecting
thirsty throats swallowing up
large quantities of water
and then some more

cups of reddened clay
passed from one hand
to the next
a discussion soon began
about a way
to acquire food
more regularly
for the lepers
whom they passed
on the way
i watched jesus
as he spoke about the conditions
of the lepers
in this room
there was a real feeling
of compassion
it was as if
a red light streaking
it was perceptible
could not move
had no desire
to flee to the kitchen
jesus
sharing how he had
spoken to one leper
called thomas
he had eight children
for twelve years
he had been marginated
from all of society
not being able to have any contact
with his family
his hands were missing

jesus' face was changed
as he spoke about this
   i wanted to ask jesus
   something
   that had been in my heart
   for so long
   and even though
   women do not ask questions
   in these settings
   i asked
      master
      why are there such divisions
      within our people?
      why do some
      in this village have so much
      and others nothing?
immediately
this began
a lively discussion
some of his disciples
expressing
for this reason
we needed to be closer
to the zealots
jesus
remaining silent
yet i could tell
he was moved
by the conversation
sitting there that afternoon
had
so many questions
to ask him

mary i can't find words
to answer your questions
but
i still have present inside me
this leper thomas
i still feel his pain
sometimes
we are called
to take the pain
into us
the capacity
for human beings
to destroy others
is tremendous
feeling
such deep compassion
flow from jesus
sitting next to him
jesus
sometimes i feel
so powerless
i would like you
to come with me
to the prison
where my friends are jailed
by the romans
jesus
sometimes
i am overwhelmed
don't know what to do
after i visit them
i think
about what i have

and feel so powerless
  feel so overwhelmed
  by suffering
jesus
could you go
with me tomorrow?
of course i'll go with you
martha
running into the room
breaking through red light
i can't do all this by myself
mary
i need your help
martha said jesus
don't you understand
it is time now
to be healed
refreshed from being so preoccupied
refreshed
with the cool water
  cooling parched mouths
feeling
difficulties
remembrances
of days past
mary listening
remembering her school friend
who was killed
by the romans last week
starting to cry
embracing jesus
jesus
i have been trying to hide

all this pain i feel
by being busy
with so many things
but that is not taking
away the pain
not at all
i just need to also sit
looking at your face jesus
i tell you
i knew samuel
since i was five
he was active
in the movement
he would take risks
no one would take
jesus
one day he was nearby here
i was on my way to visit friends
i saw the romans
capture him and his two friends
they were smuggling weapons
the soldiers did not even
take them to prison
for this crime
they shoved each one
to the ground
and beat them to death
long deep sobs
surfaced from within
gasping for air
the violence
the cruelty of this act
was felt in this room

moving jesus deeply
jesus thank you
for listening to me
i feel better
telling you this
i have been keeping
all this inside
for too long
on some level
feel you are healing me
the sound of the beatings
the cries before the final moment
the flowing out of blood
the red staining the ground
jesus
i can't live with those memories
i need you to help me
to heal them
heal me
jesus
taking all this in
deep
deep places within
being touched
being healed
thank you jesus
for passing through our door
and coming into
this inner room

stones

john 8:1–11

As for Jesus, he went to the Mount of Olives.

At daybreak Jesus appeared in the Temple again. All the people came to him, and he sat down and began to teach them.

Then the teachers of the Law and the Pharisees brought in a woman who had been caught in the act of adultery. They made her stand in front of everyone. "Master," they said, "this woman has been caught in the act of adultery. Now the Law of Moses orders that such women be stoned to death; but you, what do you say?" They said this to test Jesus, in order to have some charge against him.

Jesus bent down and started writing on the ground with his finger. And as they continued to ask him, he straightened up and said to them, "Let the man among you who has no sin be the first to throw a stone at her." And he bent down again, writing on the ground.

As a result of his words, they went away, one by one, starting with the oldest, and Jesus was left alone with the woman standing before him. Then Jesus stood up and said to her, "Woman, where are they? Has no one condemned you?" She replied, "No one." And Jesus said, "Neither do I condemn you; go away and don't sin again."

it was light years ago
my father had died suddenly
soon my mother was with another man
i can still see his face
he abused me so much
my mother always defended him
i was forced to run away
when i was eleven
i began this living when i arrived
at this lake town
at first i hated myself
   i hated what i was doing
soon i felt nothing
making enough to stay alive
i would be going once again
where the rich of the town lived
where the owners of the large boats dwelt
i was with the owner
of the largest fleet
of fishing boats
suddenly the door
to our room was swung wide open
his wife and her brother a pharisee
peered upon us
soon they were dragging me
from the room
while the man they caught me with
just walked out the door
i always had feared
this would happen to me
and i would be dragged

where they stoned persons
like me to death
the man walking away free
as if he had done nothing wrong
images of my stepfather were strong
   in my mind
childhood memories broke through
my frozen heart
a tremendous sadness choking me
more painful than being publicly dragged
through town as a sinner
all these religious smiling
above me
as if they had just caught
a good catch from the lake
if they only knew
what my life had been like
if they only knew
where were they when i needed help?
where were they when i needed
someone to help me break out
of this cycle? where?
soon arriving at the place
they would soon crush me
with their hate
as if they had never committed
sins against yahweh
why must i be the excuse
for them to feel so pure?
   so holy?
the wife of the man with whom i was
raised her self-righteous voice
this woman is worth nothing

she is a common prostitute
according to our law
she must be stoned
we could be lenient
but we must let her
be an example
to our daughters
her behavior is intolerable
as she spoke
i could remember
how many of my poor friends
told me
how she treated them
in her luxurious house
if they broke something
she would beat them
as if they were dogs
she put money
in the synagogue's box
and did all the ablutions
for this reason
she considered herself
so holy pure close to god
but lying
with my face
against the ground
i wondered
who the holy and unholy ones are
i was wondering what yahweh felt
about all this
a voice cuts hers off
i looked up
i saw his face

his truth was so strong
these hypocrites froze
in their condemning
he looked at me
with much understanding
he spoke calmly
looking at each one
standing over me
with their heavy rocks
ready to kill
so you are ready to condemn this woman
because all of you are so holy
your outsides are so clean
you obey all the laws to be pure
i tell you this day
yahweh does not care about the external
he cares about the heart
what our heart is like
look at this one here
ready to thrust her stone
and crack open the head of maria here
bending down writing on the earth
look within your own heart
do you think you are better than others
because of your money or status?
how do you treat your workers?
your hearts are full of worms
your hate is destroying you
one by one
jesus wrote on the ground
not what appeared to be superficial
but what was really in the heart
soon i was alone

with this one
he lifted me up
took me into his arms
felt at that moment
i could change
he was healing me
of my past
i could feel
jesus felt bad
what had been done to me
i didn't need to say one word
his unconditional love
swept over
years of abuse
years of self-hate
felt as if
i was being born again

humility

luke 18:9–14

Jesus told another parable to some persons fully convinced of their own righteousness, who look down on others, "Two men went up to the Temple to pray; one was a Pharisee and the other a tax collector. The Pharisee stood by himself and said: 'I thank you, God, that I am not like other people, grasping, crooked, adulterous, or even like this tax collector. I fast twice a week and give the tenth of all my income to the Temple.'

"In the meantime the tax collector, standing far off, would not even lift his eyes to heaven, but beat his breast saying: 'O God, be merciful to me, a sinner.'

"I tell you, when this man went down to his house, he was reconciled with God, but not the other. For whoever makes himself out to be great will be humbled, and whoever humbles himself will be raised higher."

there had been much business
  in jerusalem
had been a very successful time
for abram
he had gained tremendously
he would go to the temple
to let everyone know
how successful he had been
at the same time
he entered
was one called samuel
a tax collector
who came to pray

as they passed
through the large polished doors
as they found themselves
inside the temple
abram went to the very front
while samuel
stayed in the back

i was with jesus
speaking about the conflicts
between groups
jesus watched
as the two men
took their places
he followed
abram to the very front
of the temple
he stood in front

of the worshipers
praying

yahweh
how good it is to be here
i look around me
i see these poor sinners
i am repulsed by these sinners
i watch these people
who come here
to be with yahweh
but all day
they commit tremendous offenses
against you
oh yahweh
i stand here happy
to be so close
to you
i am also happy
that i keep
perfectly your precepts
   laws
how difficult it must be
for a sinner
like that tax collector
behind me

i watched the face of jesus
he was shocked by the arrogance
of this pharisee
downcast face
jesus walked to the back
of the temple
where samuel was seated

his prayer was so different
from abram's
praying simply
yahweh
i am sorry
for what i have done wrong
i am not worthy
of your time
please bear with me
as i try to change

we walked out of the shadow
of the temple
into the light of the day
jesus came over
where samuel was
asking him to pass
some time with us
jesus asking samuel
if he came often
to the temple
and it was clear
that samuel was hesitant
jesus
speaking clearly
yahweh seeks you out
loves you as you are
your humility is moving
knowing this
i ask you
if you would like
to join our group
i see something great

in you
and could contribute
much to our work
samuel looked shocked
could not believe his ears
jesus you saw me
in this temple
i am afraid to even
speak with yahweh
feel unworthy
and you ask me
to join a work
dedicated to yahweh
but being with you jesus
i feel empowered
to do something great
for yahweh
from that day forward
samuel stayed with jesus
in spite of the difficulties
it was the happiest time
in his life
abram returned home
became richer more arrogant
died soon after of gluttony
his arrogance prevented him
from meeting jesus
two men entered the temple
one thinking he owned yahweh
lost terribly
the other feeling his smallness
before god
received everything

transfiguration

luke 9:28–36

About eight days after Jesus had said all this, he took Peter, John and James and went up the mountain to pray. And while he was praying, the aspect of his face was changed and his clothing became dazzling white. Two men were talking with Jesus, Moses and Elijah. They had just appeared in heavenly glory and were telling him about his departure that had to take place in Jerusalem.

Peter and his companions had fallen asleep, but they awoke suddenly and saw Jesus' Glory and the two men standing with him. As Moses and Elijah were about to leave, Peter said to him, "Master, how good it is for us to be here for we can make three tents, one for you, one for Moses and one for Elijah." For Peter didn't know what to say. And no sooner had he spoken than a cloud appeared and covered them; and the disciples were afraid as they entered the cloud. Then these words came from the cloud, "This is my Son, my Chosen one, listen to him." And after the voice had spoken, Jesus was there alone.

The disciples kept this to themselves at the time, telling no one of anything they had seen.

it was early morning
it was completely dark
we were lying on our backs
staring up at the stars
soon the sun would be up
this desert terrain
would be warmed
looked over
and jesus was awake
also gazing at stars
slip across the early morning sky
jesus
turning to me
asking me if i would like
to go with him to pray
to the top of the mountain
looked at the darkened silhouette
jesus
are you sure
you have the energy
to climb to the top?
it is going to take us
at least three hours
but jesus
we are always stuck
here at the base
we never
make the time
for this climb
jesus
let's go before everyone

wakes up
plus jesus
i would love to pray
with you
we silently slipped away
with john and james
taking enough water and food
till the afternoon
felt good walking with jesus
we found the path
right away
with the help of the full moon
when jesus needed
to get away
he began to talk
as we slowly watched
the horizon lighten
as the stars slid beyond
jesus began to ask us
if we thought
anyone understood his message?
were people just wanting magic?
or did they really desire
a closer union with yahweh?
with one another
in this project
to build a better world?
telling jesus
how hard it was for all of us
to understand
we had been used to living
from the external
in obeying laws

his way was different
it was all about the way
of the heart
the desires that bring us
close to yahweh and his reign
jesus looking serious
relying heavily on his walking stick
his eyes gazing out
to the distance
watching the sun
slowly rise above the hills
another day
slowly working our way
to the top
enjoying watching jesus unwind
sun up above us
as we reached the top
felt so good
to finally be here
looking out
on such vastness
feeling a freedom
being in this spot
sitting down eating the bread
salted fish
enjoying each other's company
suddenly
as the storms
that erupt on the sea of galilee
i felt a sleepiness
overpower me
jesus asking me if i wanted
to pray with him

i told him yes
but sleep won
falling into the oblivion
of unconsciousness
asleep for an hour
suddenly awakening looking up
gazing in front
saw jesus standing
there was something happening
i was being pulled
into deep mystery
feeling a tremendous sacredness
about the moment
tried to say something
but couldn't
just moved closer to where
jesus was
a strong luminousness
flowed from him
the depths of who jesus is
being revealed to us
in this encounter
looking up
feeling others with us
was afraid at first
this all was too much
hearing this is my beloved son
listen to him
same words
i heard when we were at the river
for his baptism
my beloved son
listen to him

hearing the words
this is my beloved son
listen to him

in front of me
jesus
there were rays of light
strong
flowing from jesus
it was also
flowing within me not sure
what was happening out there
and what was happening inside me
feeling connected
immersed
overwhelmed
by something
  someone greater
stretching all my ideas
pulling me into new terrain
light bright
illuminating
flowing

jesus
would like to stay
here forever
with this experience
feel a joy a peace
never thought possible
thinking of all the people
we had seen this week
broken diseased
all these sad stories

also in me
letting this bright light
this power from jesus
also touch
those who i carried with me
as i prayed
on this mountaintop
asking jesus
to also let this light
touch the sick boy
that came to the house yesterday
his stomach inflated
the sadness the sorrow
in the eyes
of his mother
jesus i ask you here
on this mountaintop
feeling the warmth
the brightness
of your otherness
that this light touch this young boy
suffering
i closed my eyes
and concentrated on seeing him
letting him
also feel this healing warmth
standing next to you jesus
here on the mountaintop
listening to your abba
feel myself lost jesus
i feel you are extending
yourself in friendship
that you want us

to know you better
by being here
feeling your presence

jesus remember back
to this morning
you asked me
if i wanted to come
with you to pray
what happens?
i fall asleep
wake up
i find myself
in new territory
feel jesus
a gratefulness
that you invited me
to know you
to know you jesus
have appreciated your friendship
your presence
feel as if you too
have gotten to know
who i am
my moods my likes dislikes
but something more
is happening this afternoon
never realized
knowing you
would push me
into this terrain
jesus
all my life

i have struggled
so hard
to know yahweh
to struggle
against so many injustices
here i find myself
being with you
not trying at all
but being swept up
in friendship
jesus
looking at me
feeling lost with these words
jesus' abba
was uttering these words
also to me
his son
the one he also takes pleasure in

deep mystery
jesus
putting his loving arm
around me
giving me strength
to pray
abba
one who made all this land
in front of us
abba
one who is at the source
of all
you are greater
than the vastness

of all of our universe
some days i feel lost
try to do
what is right
but i feel this morning
something else
when i work
for you
when i accompany your son
visiting the sick
those who are in jail
that jesus says
this also gives you pleasure
abba
that somehow
these actions
are touching you
thank you
for letting me know
what i do
truly affects you
thank you

children

mark 10:13-16

People were bringing their little children to him to have him touch them, and the disciples rebuked them for this.

When Jesus noticed it, he was very angry and said, "Let the children come to me and don't stop them, for the kingdom of God belongs to such as these. Truly I say to you, whoever does not receive the kingdom of God like a child will not enter it." Then he took the children in his arms and laying his hands on them, blessed them.

it was early morning
the day had not begun
yesterday was a tense day
with the conflicts with the pharisees
   i sat staring at the water
   from the jordan
   flow over rocks
   watching green leaves
   whirl around and around
   in the wind
reflecting back
   when i first saw jesus
then when i introduced myself
he invited me
to pass the afternoon
with him
we talked about so many things
time has passed quickly
since then
in the distance
catching sight
of a group of mothers
with their children
running laughing
jesus was always
being asked
for so many things
under the tree
knew how exhausted
he was when he fell asleep
last night

mothers now in front of me
we would like to get
   a blessing from jesus
   for our children
   they are going to begin
   their studies
   we need jesus' help
felt impatient
friends
can't you see
jesus is fast asleep
do you have any idea
how hard he works?
the long hours
and you want to bother him
for a blessing
for your children?

impossible
out of the question
don't even think
for a moment this can happen
suddenly the air
was let out of the ball
deflated heads
hung low
in that moment
jesus awakening
joining us
   can i help you?
   he utters suddenly
   there was reborn joy
   in the faces of the mothers

jesus we have come here
to ask you
if you would be so generous
   to bless our children
of course i will
jesus asked each one
to come over
he sat down
   he took two young ones
   into his arms
   embracing them
our abba
   desires so many good things
   for you
may you use
   the intelligence our abba
   has given you
young ones
   asking jesus questions
   about yahweh
   how to get closer
jesus
   taking his hands
   placing them
   over their heads
   asking
   his abba
   to fill them
   with his love
   to protect them from harm

how important to enjoy
the moment

lepers

matthew 8:1-4

When Jesus came down from the mountain, large crowds followed him.

Then a leper came forward. He knelt before him and said, "Sir, if you want to, you can make me clean." Jesus stretched out his hand, touched him, and said, "I want to, be clean again." At that very moment the man was cleansed from his leprosy. Then Jesus said to him, "See that you do not tell anyone, but go to the priest, have yourself declared clean, and offer the gift that Moses ordered as proof of it."

it was early
in the morning
my friends told me
that one who heals
   will be in capernaum
   i did not have hope
   had lost all my hope
   how many days
   had i prayed for yahweh
   to heal me
   so i could return to my family?
my skin burned at night
part of my hands
were missing
lonely living so far away
from the ones i love
   could i ask
   one more time
   to be healed?
   why did this
   happen to me?
i have always
tried to love yahweh
with my whole heart
   whole mind
   whole soul
one day waking up
my skin burning
how many days and nights
have i suffered?
pain shooting through my body

many times
seeing my wife and kids
in the distance
not able to visit them
   to touch them
   i was an outcast
   by law
always ringing my bell
announcing
an unclean person
even worse than a sinner
how my heart
was torn apart
by this pain
and today
was i willing
to ask once again
to be healed?
to be part of my family again?
walking with my other friends
one step after the other
trying to find some hope
within
to be healed
walking toward
one who heals
walking over rocky dusty road
in the distance
could see it was the one
we were told about
he was speaking
on top of a small hill
his voice floating

through the air
catching me off guard
losing my breath
i found myself
with the strength
of this voice
telling myself
maybe today
but i knew i needed to ask
i grabbed on to the power
i found in this voice
to ask to be healed
even before i neared this one
named jesus
i said out loud
please one greater
touch me
for too long
i have felt my skin
burn
i feel i am being destroyed
i am hardly human
one greater
please touch me
i am asking you
we almost ran
to where jesus stood
i had a small wave of hope
jesus
we have come here
to ask you to touch us
to heal us
we have suffered for so long

please come near us
and heal us
we didn't want to come
because we have asked
so many times
and we still suffer
are outcasts
jesus
putting his hands
on my shoulders
so many times
life did not make sense
seemed so unfair
but feeling the weight
of jesus' hand
i felt at peace
for the first time
in years
someone had touched me
jesus
i am asking you
with my whole heart
to heal me
i closed my eyes
full of bright light
inside
feeling this healing presence
of this one
deep within
in this moment
being connected to jesus
felt the darkness
the suffering of these past years

being healed
by this light
the loneliness the rejection
i had felt
for so long
the meaninglessness of life
i could see
all those wounds disappear inside
felt a warmth
flowing from jesus' hands
healing the oozing wounds
breathing in deep
feeling strong this healing
a sensation in my whole body
of being made whole
opening my eyes
looking into the eyes
of the one
who gave me hope
jesus
thank you
for letting me
first hear your voice
giving me courage
to come before you
for not despising me
because i was ugly
to look at
oozing with puss
sores everywhere
i see in you
an understanding
i have never found

anywhere else
jesus
i am grateful
for your healing power
may i never lack
the courage to ask you
again
for your deep healing light

zaccheus

luke 19:1–10

When Jesus entered Jericho and was going through the city, a man named Zaccheus was there. He was a tax collector and a wealthy man. He wanted to see what Jesus was like, but he was a short man and could not see because of the crowd. So he ran ahead and climbed up a sycamore tree. From there he would be able to see Jesus who had to pass that way. When Jesus came to the place, he looked up and said to him, "Zaccheus, come down quickly for I must stay at your house today." So Zaccheus hurried down and received him joyfully.

All the people who saw it began to grumble and said, "He has gone to the house of a sinner as a guest." But Zaccheus spoke to Jesus, "The half of my goods, Lord, I give to the poor, and if I have cheated anyone, I will pay him back four times as much." Looking at him Jesus said, "Salvation has come to this house today, for he is also a true son of Abraham. The Son of Man has come to seek and to save the lost."

it had been a long day
too long
so many problems with so many pilgrims
entering the city
arriving home
no one there
just seems
with money
everyone is so much busier
never time for each other
felt an emptiness
entering
into the luxurious gathering room
heard
loud noises outside
as if returning armies
loud cries
pounding feet

there was nothing
inside here for me
so i opened the wooden door
saw a large crowd
approaching
hearing
the name of jesus
being repeated
over and over again

i had heard
so many stories
about jesus

as i collected taxes
from the poor
what was
i looking for
in life?
i know
i had not experienced it
in the emptiness
of my house
with relationships so superficial
searching for something
knowing
i would never be able
to see jesus
if i stayed
where i was
ran a distance
knowing
i needed
to climb the tree
in order
to catch a glimpse
of jesus
thought
it was worth it
just had heard
so many amazing things
about him
   i was anxious
climbing the tree
felt that i could fall
but i knew it would be worth it
looking out

into the distance
as far as i could see
were long stretches of sand
tops of palm trees
being blown
by the warm desert wind
so many thoughts
passed through my mind
as i gazed
out into the distance
remembering
how i had fallen
into this type of work
which i hated
how
i had lost so many friends
how each day
seemed as if it
would never end
and now i was hoping
that something would happen today
climbing higher up the tree
how was i ever
going to climb down?
it seemed
impossible to get
out of my life
the pressures the demands
looking ahead
as the crowd approached
saw in the group
many of my neighbors
many of the people

with whom
i made enemies
during these years
saw many of the people
i had unjustly
collected taxes from
during the morning
they can't see me like this
then i saw jesus
he was carrying a small child
on his shoulders
   i almost fell from
   the heights of the tree
   my hand grabbed
   hard the broken branch
   what
   was happening to me?
i watched jesus
as he stopped
and spoke with the old man
who always
puts his cup
out to beg
because he is blind
jesus
didn't hurry by him
rather
   he bent down
   put a coin into the cup
   started to talk to him
   reflecting
   how i treat people
   how i always think

    i am superior
    to those
who don't have what i have
wondering
if i am not
the most miserable of all
jesus seemed
to enjoy himself
with the people
he was journeying with
i wish
i was not shut out
from the community
i could
also walk with jesus
but that would be
impossible
because of who
i am
jesus nearing
the tree where i was
glad i was high enough
and hidden enough
that i would not be recognized
jesus
standing below the tree
looking up
to where i was
he looked into my eyes
again i felt
i was going to fall
fall and be destroyed
zaccheus

come down
i am going
to eat with you
in your home
jesus
was talking to me
my neighbors
don't talk to me
no one talks to me
i am considered impure
   a sinner
   here jesus
   the one everyone
   says is close to yahweh
   is addressing me
something is not right
   what did
   you say master?
i said
   i know you are short
   and if you
   want to see me
   meet me
   i'm hungry
   i've traveled all day
i would like to share
a meal with you
shocked sound vibrated
through the crowd
but i didn't pay attention
letting go
of the branch
letting go

of the person
who i used to be
so concerned
about my image
i slipped
down the base of the tree
stood on the ground
grounded at last
looked up
into the understanding eyes
of jesus
was the first time
in my life
i did not feel short
felt accepted
for who i am
felt new places
opening up within
i was not short
in the eyes of jesus
i was who i am
a person
accepted by this holy man
this unconditional love
permitted me
   to announce
that tomorrow i would
donate half of my wealth
to build houses for lepers
and all the people
   i had cheated
   i would generously return
   their money

i would sell my home
and begin again
in what i was trained in
a teacher
i was just too greedy
because
i didn't make enough
in this profession
looked at jesus
as i spoke
my heart felt warm
my heart felt new
didn't care
what all these
judgmental people
thought
i reached up
and embraced jesus
uttering
jesus
how can i thank you
enough
i was lost in my house
only a few moments before
now i am someone
different
all my life
i have had people
laugh at me
because i was short
i felt bad about myself
i thought
if i were rich enough

people would respect me
but none of that
has made me happy
what i have found
in your acceptance
jesus
is i am loved
just as i am
jesus
thank you for
letting me
be
who i am
and not what
others tell me
accepted
and loved
by you
thank you
jesus

pharisees

luke 14:1 – 6

One Sabbath Jesus had gone to eat a meal in the house of a leading Pharisee, and he was carefully watched. In front of him was a man suffering from dropsy; so Jesus asked the teachers of the Law and the Pharisees, "Is it lawful to heal on a Sabbath or not?" But no one answered. Jesus then took the man, healed him and sent him away. And he addressed them, "If your lamb or your ox falls into a well on a Sabbath day, who among you doesn't hurry to pull him out?" And they could not answer.

it was the day
before the sabbath
everyone was hurrying
trying to finish
everything
before sundown
  jesus came over
  to our group
  he did not seem
  to be rushed
  he sat down
  talking about
  many things
we were near
the temple
this solid structure
pharisees
rushing by
when i recognized
david
who had a terrible
skin disease
which had left
him blind
he had fallen
from the walkway
to the temple
and was crying
for help
the pharisees saw him
then said out loud

sorry we cannot
  stop
   we need to
   find three items
   before sunset
we could never
do anything on
   the sabbath
so busy
so preoccupied
in doing
our cleaning rituals
david
look at what
time it is
we'll send someone
to help you
jesus was taking
all this in
now watching
two sadducees hurrying
by david
sacred scrolls written
about yahweh
and his relationship
with his people
hurrying so fast
that when david
yelled out for help
they glanced
at him
and told him
that they were sorry

but they needed
to keep
their hands clean
to carry
yahweh's word
jesus and our group
walking
over to where
david fell
jesus asking david
if he was all right
that they would find
a ladder
looking about
seeing a ladder
at one of the booths
borrowing it
from a woman
selling fruit
lowering it
to where david was
jesus himself
lowering himself
to help david up
relief
spread across his face
returning
to our spot
where we were
sitting
around in a circle
why is everyone
rushing so fast

they miss
where yahweh is?
so concerned
about the external
while the most important
they miss
slowing down
sometimes
helps us
to see
what is most important
sitting there
listening to jesus
feeling
the power
coming from him
i asked him
jesus
how do we do this?
our law tells us
we cannot do many things
on the sabbath
plus i personally
have so many obligations
jesus
how can we avoid
rushing by
people in need
like david?
jesus looked at me
asking me
what
did i most desire?

was anything worth
blocking this desire?
walk
do not let
all these external pressures
dominate you
walk
don't run so fast
or you will miss
the most important
thing in life
looking how content
david was
sitting with our group
knew jesus was right
not to be driven
by these external forces
so that we miss
moments like this
being with a brother
in need

multiplication

john 6:1-11

After this Jesus went to the other side of the Sea of Galilee, near Tiberias, and large crowds followed him because of the miraculous signs they saw when he healed the sick. So he went up into the hills and sat down there with his disciples. Now the Passover, the feast of the Jews, was at hand.

Then lifting up his eyes, Jesus saw the crowds that were coming to him and said to Philip, "Where shall we buy bread so that these people may eat?" He said this to test Philip, for he himself knew what he was going to do. Philip answered him, "Two hundred silver coins would not buy enough bread for each of them to have a piece."

Then one of Jesus' disciples, Andrew, Simon Peter's brother, said, "There is a boy here who has five barley loaves and two fish; but what good are these for so many?"

Jesus said, "Make the people sit down." There was plenty of grass there so the people, about five thousand men, sat down to rest. Jesus then took the loaves, gave thanks and distributed them to those who were seated. He did the same with the fish and gave them as much as they wanted.

i left school
when i was eight
my father drank
there were six of us
i began to work
every morning i would go
to the lake of capernaum
i would help the fishermen
clean the fish
freshly caught
this morning
my mother insisted
i accompany her
to listen to a teacher
from nazareth
i didn't want to go
i hated religious things
i had seen too much misery
to believe in the words
addressed to yahweh
i relied on myself
that was enough
for three days
i had sat
with my family
listening to jesus
what he said
seemed to make sense
but i was too cynical
after seeing
how my father beat my mother

how the poor don't have
enough to eat
while the rich
have too much
i was glad
i had packed
my salty fish
glad
i could care for my family
it was evening
this one
asked the crowd
if anyone had brought food
i clutched my fish
close to me
i couldn't let go of this
gazing up at this one
a campesino from nazareth
something began to melt inside
my bitterness broke through
enough
to wander up
to where jesus
was speaking
i carried the fish
in my bag
i looked at jesus
ezekiel
thank you for coming here
i know
it was hard
for you to trust
to share your fish

but it is time
to let go
of all the hardships
you have endured
you are young
but with a bitter heart
give over to me
along with your fish
the memories
that are paralyzing you
i began to sob
uncontrollably
jesus
knelt next to me
put his arms
around me
i was not aware
of anyone else
i just let out
all the pain
i had been carrying
ever since i could remember
felt jesus
was taking this suffering
that flowed out of me
memories images
burst forth from my heart
flowed out
in streams of tears
jesus bringing me
close to his heart
beating gently
learn from me

i am gentle of heart
give me your sorrow
i will transform it
to empower you
looked into jesus' eyes
a vast world opened
as he too
let tears fall slowly
on barren ground
jesus
i did not want
to come here
i had given up hope
i feel so different now
giving over to you
how i have been hurt
thank you jesus
i don't want to forget
your face
your embrace
your acceptance
giving me power
to let go
to be healed
realized i never again
want to hold on to
deep wounds
but rather
let your healing power
reach deep
into these places
standing up
with jesus

jesus handing me
the bag of fish
blessing it
i moved
among the crowd
that afternoon
reaching in
bringing out sufficient fish
for each group gathered
looking into the faces
as i handed them the fish
i understood
something more
about this one
who healed me
i saw in these faces
the same brokenness
i had experienced
i saw many of the people
who are not allowed
into the synagogue
who are considered impure
outcasts
rejects of society
always causing problems
looked
into the faces
of women who had worked
long hours
toiling under the sun
saw so many
still suffering from diseases
disabilities almost total

how did they ever
reach this out-of-the-way place?
but
there was hope
in their eyes
i could tell
they had experienced
the same healing
i had with this one
my heart
was moved
that afternoon
as i shared the fish
with these poor folks
who had been beaten down
all their lives
stepped upon
by the powerful
with those who have
the resources
the comforts
i experienced something
that afternoon
that i had never felt before
as these wounded began
to eat together
there was a sound
so subtle
i began to hear
music of brothers and sisters
sharing a meal together
music flowing from the heart
of the one who made all

music chords of perfect harmony
that it is worth it
what jesus
showed me that afternoon
was that it is difficult
fighting
to stay alive
but if we join hands
in this struggle
and share
what we have
we begin to live differently
that afternoon
there was enough to eat
felt glad
i could share with these friends
who are not welcomed
in most places
were generously welcomed
by this powerful preacher
jesus
never want to forget
the music
of the poor
sharing food together

lazarus

john 11:1–44

As for Mary, when she came to the place where Jesus was and saw him, she fell at his feet and said, "*Lord,* if you had been here, my brother would not have died." When Jesus saw her weeping and the Jews also who had come with her, he was moved in the depths of his spirit and troubled. Then he asked, "Where have you laid him?" They answered, "*Lord,* come and see." And Jesus wept.

The Jews said, "See how he loved him!" But some of them said, "If he could open the eyes of the blind man, could he not have kept this man from dying?"

Jesus was deeply moved again and drew near to the tomb. It was a cave with a stone laid across it. Jesus ordered, "Take the stone away." Martha said to him, "*Lord,* by now he will smell, for this is the fourth day." Jesus replied, "Have I not told you that if you believe, you will see the glory of God?" So they removed the stone.

Jesus lifted his eyes and said, "Father, I thank you for you have heard me. I know that you hear me always; but my prayer was for the sake of these people, that they may believe that you sent me." When Jesus had said this, he cried out in a loud voice, "Lazarus, come out!"

The dead man came out, his hands and feet bound with linen strips and his face wrapped in a cloth. So Jesus said to them, "Untie him and let him go."

jesus why have you taken
so long to come here?
why?
i believe that my brother
would still be alive
if you had come earlier
why did you take so long?
jesus
being moved by martha's crying
expressing her grief
at her brother's death
an empty feeling
filling jesus' interior
loss of a friend
many thoughts
passing through jesus' heart
remembering
so many times
passing long hours
at the table
conversing with lazarus
jesus burying his face
between his hands
tears flowing hard
through his hands
feeling great sorrow
an emptiness
death
jesus seeing the face
of death
death for so many

as the ultimate enemy
losing everything
no longer present
absence
enemy
destroying all
jesus
staying in this moment
feeling something else
flowing through him
a sliver of light
vibrating
eternal life
life that does not end
light
at the end of the tunnel
how death
is not the ultimate answer
this sliver of life
eternal life
feeling the depth of this
same feeling
jesus had
under
the water during his baptism
darkness
letting go
falling down a steep cliff
trusting
in his abba's hand
who would catch him
feeling under the water
how his life

would be connected to conquering death
so that whoever knows his abba
would never die
falling down
being caught by
one who loves us
without limits
falling down
caught
held by one greater
not being smashed
on the ground
life without end
feeling this life
feeling eternity
at the same time
listening
to the screams
of the wailers
the anguish of many
surrounding us
recounting the great deeds
of lazarus
how deeply this friend
was loved
for this reason
the sorrow so great
being expressed
jesus also feeling
this sorrow
feeling grief
and hope
at the same time

hands wet with tears
walking
toward the tomb
how important
to see
how all this
is not permanent
it is all
so fleeting passing
how
we are on pilgrimage
important
not to try
to hold on
to this life
rather give your life away
don't accumulate
don't try to possess
jesus
knowing all this
but still his heart
felt
    like being in a long stretch of desert
    alone and lost
    tears wetting barren earth
standing
in front of a tomb
the group feeling the loss
of a good and close friend
jesus looking about
    praying
    abba
    our hearts are sorrowful

we no longer
see in front of us
our loving friend
now an emptiness
romans
try to tell us
that everything is over at death
that is why
it is important
to live for the moment
but our friend lazarus is alive
death is not an enemy
to show our friends here
how those who follow
a path of love
of service
who try to share
and believe in you abba
will never die
impossible
i ask you
to touch lazarus
let the people here
feel
how those who have gone before
are still with you
just as people of faith
always feel the dead close
so this afternoon
abba
i pray that we might grow in
our faith
when we actually see lazarus again

how close the dead
are to us
help us
so when we lack this faith
blind to this other dimension
of life
we will believe
we thank you abba
that the dead
have eternal life
go on living
and are still part
of our lives
lazarus come forth

foot washing

john 13:1-9

It was before the feast of the Passover. Jesus realized that his hour had come to pass from this world to the Father, and as he had loved those who were his own in the world, he would love them with the perfect love.

They were at supper; the devil had already put into the mind of Judas, son of Simon Iscariot, to betray him, but Jesus knew that the Father had entrusted all things to him, and as he had come from God, he was going to God. So he got up from table, removed his garment and taking a towel, wrapped it around his waist. Then he poured water into a basin and began to wash his disciples' feet and wipe them with the towel he was wearing.

When he came to Simon Peter, Simon said to him, "Why, *Lord*, you want to wash my feet!" Jesus said, "What I am doing you cannot understand now, but afterwards you will understand it." Peter replied, "You shall never wash my feet."

Jesus answered him, "If I do not wash you, you can have no part with me." Then Simon Peter said, "*Lord*, wash not only my feet, but also my hands and my head."

darkness covering the entrance
to the room
everything was prepared
candles lighting the places
slowly my friends
entering the room
wearing a look of concern
i was feeling
how i had liked working
with them
trying to build our project
now it was time
to celebrate the passover
rising from the table
taking a towel
next to me
removing robe
kneeling down with water basin
in front of peter
jesus
what are you doing?
you can't wash my feet
this is what we should do for you
looking at jesus
remembering during these years
all the times together
working hard
the times on the hillside
when so many sick
would approach jesus
to be healed

he felt the pain
of these sick
   you could tell
   he felt this
   as he bent over
   and cured
   the way in which
   he touched those in need
   it always seemed
   someone wanted something
   always wanting his help
demands
would fly at jesus
from all directions
sometimes
i don't know
how he did it
   remember so well
   how jesus
   dealt with death
   lazarus was in the tomb
   jesus cared for him
   i remember talking to him
   about death
   that conversation will always
   stay with me
   after that i was not afraid
   of death as before
   i had seen
   so many people die
   during these years
   there was a terror about it
   but jesus changed this

now he was taking
my feet into his hands
wanting to wash them
pouring warm water
dirt flowing off
washing my feet

jesus
why are you doing this?
feeling the mystery
the power of this one
rubbing off the dirt
i need to do this peter
   you need to know
   how to work
   to take the last seat
   to be the servant
   not to always try to win
   but work together
   washing each other's feet
as jesus was saying this
i felt a love strong
for the one touching my feet
felt in that moment
something happened within
the heart opening
not able to say anything
jesus
i have been with you
all during these years
i have walked with you
seen you confront the powerful
seen you cure the most marginated

i think
what i am feeling
looking at you now
washing my feet
is a strong love
that is connected
to your abba
as if red rays of light
flowing from your hands
into my heart
now bursting over
i love you jesus
tears warm
flowing down my cheeks
mixing in
with the water
in the basin
how hard to be alive
jesus
how hard
to know
what we are to do
but the feeling in this moment
is i really do love you
and only
because you first loved me
jesus
looking at me
feeling how totally lost
i was
taking me
into his arms
feeling jesus close

red burning currents
of love
feeling how
beautiful you are jesus
jesus whatever happens
as long as i live
i will remember this moment
that wherever i go
whatever project i take on
i will do
because i love you
more than anyone
don't know what all this means
but my heart is
expanding
just know that i want to do
what i do
out of love for you
feeling jesus very happy
at what i was saying
and jesus
the times when i am
so exhausted
when nothing makes sense
when i feel alone
when it all seems useless
let me remember back
to this moment
as you wash my feet
embracing me
teaching me
to be a servant
and i tell you jesus

you are beautiful
more than i have ever felt
tumbling down inner chambers
loved by you
may this feeling
always remain with me

agony

matthew 26:36 – 44

Jesus came with them to a place called Gethsemane, and he said to his disciples, "Sit here while I go over to pray."

He took Peter and the two sons of Zebedee along with him, and he began to be filled with anguish and distress. And he said to them, "My soul is filled with sorrow even to death. Remain here and stay awake with me."

He went a little farther and fell to the ground, with his face touching the earth, and prayed, "Father, if it is possible, take this cup away from me. Yet not what I want, but what you want." He went back to his disciples and found them asleep, and he said to Peter, "Could you not stay awake with me for even an hour? Stay awake and pray, so that you may not slip into temptation. The spirit indeed is eager, but human nature is weak."

He again went away and prayed, "Father, if this cup cannot be taken away from me without my drinking it, let your will be done." When he came back to his disciples, he again found them asleep, for they could not keep their eyes open. He left them and again went to pray the third time, saying the same words.

finishing the meal
i could feel
a heaviness as candles were blown out
i wanted to follow
the group out
so i volunteered
to carry the water jar
no one ever took me
seriously
because i was only twelve
i had been moved
by the master's words
there had been
a deep intimacy tonight
desired
to be with jesus
with this group
for longer
even though
i knew it could be dangerous
to be seen with this group
but after sharing
bread and wine
felt strengthened
felt more connected
leaving the room secretly
a hushed tense feeling
stayed close to jesus
was not surprised
when the group
made its way to the garden

could tell
jesus was worried
preoccupied
about something approaching
asking peter and john
to stay awake
he needed their support
watched
as they withdrew
close by
jesus went over
to his normal praying place
deep in prayer
moving closer
   abba don't leave me alone
   sometimes
   i have felt
   abba my whole life
   has been a failure
   what have i achieved?
   feel down
   by the constant contradiction
   always seems
   that someone wants something
   i am afraid
   of what is going
   to happen
   if we follow
   this course
there must be an easier way
a way that
is not so costly
can have more success

why does it seem abba
we are failing?
  not making any difference
  to anyone?
  watching
  as jesus was offered
  the chalice
  sweat pouring from his forehead
  drops of blood
  wetting the ground
  abba
isn't there any other way
than to give your life away?

jesus rose
and trembling stumbled to
  where john and peter were
both of them asleep
please i need you
i feel that the powers of death
are strong
there is a sadness
fear strong
peter john
looking repentant
jesus saying
couldn't you help me out
just for this short time?
jesus returning
to his place of prayer
again the chalice
being offered
jesus

taking it into his hands
drinking wine
flowing down his mouth
the suffering the pain
of many
were contained
in that chalice
and i was the only one
who saw
how much jesus
suffered
committing himself
to drink that chalice
felt bad for jesus
went over
to where
he was dripping with blood
sat next to him
putting my arm
around him
to give your life away
feeling the liquid
as it flowed
from the chalice

blood from all those
who desire
to give their lives away
are crushed because of it
also feeling this same loneliness
as jesus does
glad i could be here jesus
know how

you are feeling alone
abandoned
a failure
use this towel
i have for the water jar
wiping his face
the towel filling with sweat and blood
help me
when i follow your path
not to be destroyed
by dark negative forces
to be accompanied by you
when all seems like a failure

veronica

luke 23:27–31

A large crowd of people followed him; among them were women beating their breast and wailing for him, but Jesus turned to them and said, "Women of Jerusalem, do not weep for me, weep rather for yourselves and for your children. For the days are coming when people will say: 'Happy are the women without child! Happy are those who have not given birth or nursed a child!' And they will say to the mountains: *Fall on us!* and to the hills: *Cover us!* For if this is the lot of the green wood, what will happen to the dry?"

jesus
healed my daughter
for thirteen years
she had lain in bed
suffering
only recently
i brought jesus
to my house
he saw my daughter
he was deeply moved
he bent down
on the mat
and put his hands
over her head
praying
she sat up
totally cured
he gave her
another chance to live
in the distance
i see it is
the same one who healed
my daughter
everyone around me
   murmuring
   that jesus is approaching
he is now near
he carries a beam
over his shoulder
he can barely walk
i look at the faces

lining the street
it is as it has been
for years
the ones who have
  all the power
the ones threatened
by jesus
are laughing at him
there is hate in their faces
they are so afraid that
what jesus
has been doing
  will influence their way of life
  what will ever change
  their hearts?
  how can they
  destroy an innocent man?
  yet they looked
  so pleased
  as if once again
  they were winning
  as if they could control the destiny
  of all
and these faces
contrasted
to faces
of ones who had been healed
moved by jesus
they were poor
from the provinces
their faces
showing the shock
  the sorrow

as they watched
how jesus was treated
the sun burned
into his body
sweat mixed with blood
dripped onto the stones
  he had helped us
  in our time of need
  now it was my time
  to respond
  i took my cloth
left the crowd
  jesus had fallen
  the guards
were approaching
i did not care
i knew
what i needed to do
i knelt down
looking into jesus'
  tortured face
they think
  this loving person
  is such
  a dangerous threat
wanted jesus
to be rid
of his sweat and blood
i gently wiped
his face
jesus i am sorry
that this is all
i can do for you

i don't understand
why they are doing this
to you
it is so unfair
it is so unfair
other women
were given courage
by this act
they also approached jesus
crying deeply
   for one
   who had done
   so much for others
   women
   who once were without hope
   jesus had given them hope
i removed the cloth
the guards were screaming at me
to move out
of the way
this one is condemned to die
i was tired
of letting everyone
walk over me
i would wait

veronica
thank you for wiping my face
this small gesture
done with great love
will be remembered

i reached over
put my hand

on jesus' shoulder
could not remain here
any longer
helped jesus up
struggling
to go forward
the soldiers once again
placing the beam
on his shoulders

pulled away
my heart broken
by this sham
this unjust deed
taking my cloth
to put back
in my bag
looked
at the imprint
jesus had left of
his face
image of the suffering
that all of us
are called to
when we follow him
a power
a love
contained so clearly
in this face
etched
on this cloth

cross

john 19:17–18

They took charge of him. Bearing his own cross, Jesus went out of the city to what it is called the Place of the Skull, in Hebrew: *Golgotha*. There he was crucified and with him two others, on either side, and Jesus was in the middle.

i needed to follow jesus
he left
the image of his face
on the cloth
with which i wiped his face
watched jesus
make the torturous journey
from the city
to the hill
he was treated
with such disdain
as if he
were an animal
his body was mutilated
as i stood
along the street
watching
a person
i have grown to love
who contained
a beauty
never known
   suffered
because this one
spoke the truth
reflecting
on all the suffering
i had seen
during this last year
it all seemed
too much

the powerful always seem
to be winning
i now stood
beneath the cross
of one
whose face i carry
on my cloth
much weaker now
slower breathing
the pain anguish
across jesus' face
was intense
jesus
so many times
i have traveled
with you
during these years
i have grown close to you
now i look
upon you
hardly human
where is yahweh in this?
jesus
all during these years
you have told us
not to run away
from suffering
when we try
to build a better world
jesus
you saw
so many things
that are wrong

your abba
always was inviting you
to enter into the center
of these injustices
jesus
you could have had
a very different kind of life
looking up
at you
nothing
  you are left
  with nothing
  no power
  no fame
  dying as a criminal
  as an undesirable
jesus
all during your life
you were always
emptying yourself
emptying yourself
as all those around you
do everything
in their power
to build up
obtain more
i never want to forget
what i am feeling now
jesus
i watched how the poor
asked so much
from you
saw the times

your heart was sad
because
the multitudes wanted
something
you couldn't give
they wanted magic
to cure everything
to be suddenly successful
that is not your way
it is slow
small steps
not dramatic
jesus
would like to relieve
your thirst
asking guards
to let me reach jesus
now jesus
i touch your face
i feel the deep gashes
where once
smooth skin
my fingers
feel the thorns
pressed into your forehead
along the side of your face
feeling your blood
jesus
feel in this moment
something more
feel a strong sense
of something more
putting my face

next to jesus'
close feeling his anguish
wetting jesus' mouth
with the sponge
the intensity of pain
something more happening

veronica
again thank you
for helping me
when i will no longer
walk with you
you will feel my absence
but also
my presence
when
you too immerse yourself
in my struggle
when people's lives are cracked open
remember
my bloodied face
next to yours
even in this emptying
something
more will be happening
i am going
to the one
who loves me
without limits
jesus
as you speak
these words
i feel a love strong

from you
telling me
how much you love us
i tell you jesus
this afternoon
that i also love you
give me strength
to continue
this journey
something more happening
climbing down the ladder
feeling an emptiness
and a love
i had never experienced before
as if this was a moment
to return to
again and again
to experience
a love
without limits
being poured out
jesus
i am grateful
i could be here
to experience this
i hope
the liquid helped
your thirst
remaining with the feeling
the power of this moment
of jesus giving over his life
emptying himself
god

breakfast

john 21:1-19

After this Jesus revealed himself to the disciples by the Lake of Tiberias. He appeared to them in this way. Simon Peter, Thomas who was called the Twin, Nathanael of Cana in Galilee, the sons of Zebedee and two other disciples were together; and Simon Peter said to them, "I'm going fishing." They replied, "We will come with you" and they went out and got into the boat. But they caught nothing that night.

When day had already broken, Jesus was standing on the shore, but the disciples did not know that it was Jesus. Jesus called them, "Children, have you anything to eat?" They answered, "Nothing." Then he said to them, "Throw the net on the right side of the boat and you will find some." When they had lowered the net, they were not able to pull it in because of the great number of fish.

Then the disciple Jesus loved said to Peter, "It's the Lord!" At his words, "It's the Lord," Simon Peter put on his clothes, for he was stripped for work, and jumped into the water. The other disciples came in the boat dragging the net full of fish; they were not far from land, about a hundred meters.

When they landed, they saw a charcoal fire with fish on it, and some bread. Jesus said to them, "Bring some of the fish you've just caught." So Simon Peter climbed into the boat and pulled the net to shore. It was full of big fish —

one hundred and fifty-three — but, in spite of this, the net was not torn.

Jesus said to them, "Come and have breakfast," and not one of the disciples dared to ask him, "Who are you?" for they knew it was the Lord. Jesus then came and took the bread and gave it to them, and he did the same with the fish.

This was the third time that Jesus revealed himself to his disciples after rising from the dead.

After they had finished breakfast, Jesus said to Simon Peter, "Simon, son of John, do you love me more than these?" He answered, "Yes, Lord, you know that I love you." And Jesus said, "Feed my lambs."

A second time Jesus said to him, "Simon, son of John, do you love me?" And Peter answered, "Yes, Lord, you know that I love you." Jesus said to him, "Look after my sheep." And a third time he said to him, "Simon, son of John, do you love me?"

Peter was saddened because Jesus asked him a third time, "Do you love me?" and he said, "Lord, you know everything; you know that I love you."

Jesus then said, "Feed my sheep. Truly, I say to you, when you were young you put on your belt and walked where you liked. But when you grow old, you will stretch out your hands and another will put a belt around you and lead you where you do not wish to go." Jesus said this to make known the kind of death by which Peter was to glorify God. And he added, "Follow me."

peter
look again at this stranger
who told us
to throw in our nets
to the right
i think it's jesus
john
of course
    jumping into the water
    splashing
    toward jesus
now in front of him
good to be in your presence

a fire in the predawn darkness
jesus had already
begun cooking breakfast
my heart was moved
by this simple detail
smelled delicious
jesus
asking me
to bring over the fish
we had just caught
walking with john
toward a large group of fish
in tangled net
a sense of hope
as dawn was slowly breaking
thought
as i entered the boat
of how different it was

a few days before
my heart was still unsure about
all that suffering
the fear the sense of loss
now this morning
feeling something
so different
gripping the ends
of the nets
streaks of red
announcing
the sun would soon
brighten the day
throwing over a net
full of fish
with john
we dragged the catch
near the fire
reflecting
how true
jesus can bring life
out of death
was good to have jesus
in our midst this morning
jesus
coming over
picking out seven
large fish
still moving frantically
the three of us
cleaning the fish
working together again
talking

without end
about these last couple of weeks
how many things
had happened
jesus now much better
with a cleaning knife
than when we first met him
could tell
he was glad
to be among us
putting fish on
the surface above the fire
putting bread on the side
everyone sitting around
the fire
watching the flames
breathing
in the freshness
of another day
aroma of cooking breakfast
looking
around at the faces
of our group
light catching their faces
many thoughts
went through my heart
with friends
in good times
and hard
helping jesus
turn the fish
  the bread
walking with the cooked fish

from one friend
to another
offering a plateful
of freshly caught fish
hot bread
watched jesus
as he handed
this plate to each friend
there was a communion
an intimacy with jesus
that he could enter
our lives
in such a simple way
know
there were memories
of so many other times
we had shared meals
how important
to be close
to share this food
to be nourished
for difficult days ahead
jesus asked me
to help him
with the passing of plates
my heart was moved
still could remember
so many times
sharing together
how good
to be connected
to these friends
looking

as jesus
handed
each one his breakfast
with care
this charcoaled fish
freshly baked bread
sitting around in the circle
jesus
so many people
enter our lives
as i look around
at the faces
of these friends
i see the faces
   of so many more
   with whom we have met
   during these years
these fish this bread
jesus
somehow i feel
this is what
you desire
us to be
food for those
we meet
something greater
happening around that fire
to become food
for others
to nourish others
serving them
emptying self
just as you have done

all your life jesus
to become food

holding the bread
in my hands
help me jesus
to be this food
to nourish others
to be eaten
to be taken for granted
and cast aside

jesus
looking at me
responding
peter
do you really desire this?
do you really love me
that much?
wait jesus
i desire to do this
not only because
i love you
and because
you are truly a friend
but just being with you
during these hours
sharing this meal
i have watched
how much
you really love
each person
sitting around this fire

do i love you?
the intensity on the faces
of my friends
do i love you?
remember jesus
many years ago
and we went
to a wedding
of your cousin in cana
still remember
what we spoke about
watching the enchantment
of the love before us
   i felt then jesus
   your love for me
   it was the first time
   jesus
   you ever told me
   you loved me
   it was
   as if yahweh
   was speaking to his people
   i felt
a closeness
an intimacy with you
   since then jesus
   i have gotten to know you
feel as if i
have been the luckiest person
in the world
to have worked alongside
of you jesus
your healing of the sick

that really touched me
there are so many people
in this land
whose lives
have been brought down low
jesus
you gave them hope
you are like bread
you give yourself
to be eaten completely
by many
jesus
i could tell you
in one sentence
how much i love you
but i did that once
when i told you
i would never leave you
rather die for you
so will not repeat that again
so rather than
jesus
than to tell you
that i love you
i tell you
that you can make
me also into bread
to be eaten
by others
know that this
being made into bread
will be difficult
to be torn apart

will try to run away
from it
but you jesus
as we sit here
watching the sun
as it appears
over these mountains
behind the lake
i ask you
to help me
   to remember this breakfast
   the joy the care
   in serving the bread
   with the fish
   everyone
   was different
   after the meal
   nourished
so jesus
rather than to tell
you i love you
i tell you
i will be bread
broken
will try to give
   my life away
glad jesus
you asked me
that question
has helped me
feel
my great affection for you
and as equally important

the consequences of this love
bread given freely
when i feel tired
   discouraged
   dark days
let me remember back
to this very moment

emmaus

luke 24:13-33

That same day, two of them were going to Emmaus, a village seven miles from Jerusalem, and they talked about what had happened. While they were talking and wondering, Jesus came up and walked with them, but their eyes were held and they did not recognize him.

He asked, "What is this you are talking about?" The two stood still, looking sad. Then one named Cleophas answered, "Why, it seems you are the only traveler in Jerusalem who doesn't know what has happened there these past few days." And he asked, "What is it?"

They replied, "It is about Jesus of Nazareth. He was a prophet, you know, mighty in word and deed before God and the people. But the chief priests and our rulers sentenced him to death. They handed him over to be crucified. We had hoped that he would redeem Israel.

It is now the third day since all this took place. It is true that some women of our group have disturbed us. When they went to the tomb at dawn, they did not find his body; they came to tell us that they had seen a vision of angels who told them that Jesus was alive. Some friends of our group went to the tomb and found everything just as the women had said, but they did not see him."

He said to them, "How dull you are, how slow of understanding! You fail to believe the message of the prophets. Is it not written that the Christ should suffer all this and then enter his glory?" Then starting with Moses and going through the prophets, he explained to them everything in Scripture concerning himself.

As they drew near the village they were heading for, Jesus made as if to go farther. But they prevailed upon him, "Stay with us, for night comes quickly. The day is now almost over." So he went in to stay with them. When they were at table, he took the bread, said a blessing, broke it and gave each a piece.

Then their eyes were opened, and they recognized him; but he vanished out of their sight. And they said to each other, "Were not our hearts filled with ardent yearning when he was talking to us on the road and explaining the Scriptures?"

They immediately set out and returned to Jerusalem. There they found the Eleven and their companions gathered together. They were greeted by these words: "Yes, it is true, the Lord is risen! He has appeared to Simon!"

Then the two told what had happened on the road and how Jesus made himself known when he broke bread with them.

we had suddenly arrived
at the inn
it would be dangerous
to continue journeying
so many thieves from these parts
did not feel tired
even though
we had covered five miles
under the hot sun
talking with this stranger
was doing something else to me
friend
would you like to join us
we are going to stay
at this inn tonight
he responded
that he was planning to go further
but instead he would join us
the three with our dusty bags
passed through the wooden doors
good to be protected
from the sun
good
to sit down
around a table
this stranger continued
to speak
i asked for some food
we were so thirsty
and hungry
i told this stranger

i could see better now
could understand
that just to judge
the events of the past days
from one dimension
would never reveal
the depths
of who god is
that the suffering
the blood flowing
the brutal torture
the mocking
was the consequence
of the master's challenging
the lies of our society
but his way of sharing
was right
is right
his death
will never take that away
never
even the way
he died
even though
it seemed our whole project
was in vain
speaking with this stranger
as we walked
along the countryside
helped me to see differently
that if god
is self-giving love
that something powerful

was happening on the cross
waiter
bringing bread and wine
sun was falling
behind small hills
looked at this stranger's face
looked at his hands
as i gave him
the bread
hands with cuts on his fingers
same type of cuts
he had on his face
he had worked hard
somewhere
light passing over his face
as i handed him the bread
feeling the cuts
feeling the connection
to the one from nazareth
who spoke of how
the powerful of this world
can never totally destroy the hope
of the poor
even though
it seems that we are always losing
know that something more
is happening
when we give our lives away
remember
seeing jesus
on the cross
i was so close to the site
cannot block

what i saw
the tremendous degradation
of jesus
jonathan and i were both there
the darkness
the bitter taste of death
and what this stranger
shared with us
as we walked this afternoon
did not take away
any of the ugliness
   of that agony
but somehow
this one gave meaning
to the worthwhileness of the struggle
he let my heart
beat fast
when he engaged us
in talking about
how in any struggle
to build a better world
you would pay the price
would suffer
he gave us
so many examples
of recent and past history
of holy men and women
who suffered greatly
who gave away
their lives
so others could live
my heart felt excited
about entering the struggle again

the setbacks the loneliness
the times
when you feel so alone
know that something more
is happening
we had been
  so discouraged
when we had left jerusalem
we had given
up hope
in the struggle
in the cause
of the poor
feeling that this stranger
had lived
what he was talking about
could not help think
that there was something
about him
that reminded me
of the master
sitting here
the three of us
around this table
with bread and wine
i was beginning to feel again
not just see again
but to let my heart
recommit not to run away
sitting around the table
i saw that is exactly
what i was doing before
running away

running away
from the conflicts
the suffering
of the struggle
i saw felt this
and at that moment of insight
this stranger
took the bread
into his hands
breaking it slowly
cut bruised fingers
gripping strongly the bread
in that moment
i peered into his face
all of a sudden
instantly
i knew i was looking at jesus
it was you jesus
who saw us so dejected
it was you jesus
who could explain scripture
could make us
once again want to continue
walking working
felt my heart overflowing
in that moment
of his hands breaking the bread
i heard
at that moment
the cries of so many victims
of persecution
heard
as jesus

broke the bread
the moans of young men
whose lives were trampled
as jesus broke the bread
heard the sobs
of young children enslaved
in work
heard the cries
of men
forced to work
under the hot sun
with little pay
as jesus broke the bread
heard the cries
of so many suffering
and what was loudest
were the cries
of those who like
you jesus
have struggled
to build a better world
where life
is not easy
where everything
is not convenient safe
   comfortable
as you break this
simple
freshly baked loaf
of bread
in your hands
jesus
i hear your own cry

and i know
that somehow
your cries and others
are connected
that the suffering
the giving of self
for something greater
is connected to you
and at that moment
i saw blood
flowing through
the cuts
in jesus' hands
and my heart
only had more love
for this one
blood flowing
connecting to all the efforts
to fight injustice
blood flowed
onto the table
flowing
connecting
giving strength
to us
not to run away
not to flee from the sacrifice
blood flowing
seeing in this instance
the same blood from the cross
feeling your presence jesus
as you break bread
that you will be with us

when
we break our lives for others
and so we can find meaning
in this breaking of bread
the love
you showed on the cross
can never be destroyed
something more
is happening
knew
my life would never be the same
feeling my hands
wet
with blood flowing
frozen
staring into the face
of this stranger
jesus
help me one greater
now to return to jerusalem
hearing jesus say
i'll be with you
i liked walking with you
you are a good person
don't give up hope
i'll be with you
and when you too
have cuts
and blood flows
from your hands
know
it is connected
to me

to life that never dies
to love
i'll be with you
look for me
feel what
you are feeling now
every time you break bread
you break your life
for another
jesus
no longer stranger
now one familiar
i tell you deeply
that i too
liked walking with you
it gave pleasure
to my heart
jesus
thank you
for breaking bread
for your blood flowing
connecting
to all
who enter the struggle
jesus . . .
then he was gone
i knew
what i must do
to where
i must return
looked at my friend
the whole place was lit
or perhaps it was just our hearts

what had happened?
we didn't speak
for what
seemed like
a very long time
now it was very late
no way
we could go back tonight
to jerusalem
but how could we keep this
to ourselves?
trying to sleep
but remembering
again and again
this stranger
turned to jesus
could see him
all night
taking the bread
into his cut hands
could see the blood flowing
could feel the price
of committing yourself
my heart was on fire
knew it would be difficult
but i wanted to follow his way
now the faint trace of light
hurrying
along the same road
as we traveled yesterday
soon approaching jerusalem
seeing troops of roman soldiers
seeing the hill

where they killed jesus
had mixed emotions
as i passed these places
but somehow
everything
was so different
after jesus walked with us
after jesus broke bread
with us
would be forever different
something
so much greater had happened
things were not ending
by crucifying jesus
they were beginning
i could feel this strong
in my heart
passing by
dried blood
hardened on the ground
at the spot where they killed jesus
saw again
the blood i had seen flowing
last evening
from jesus' hands
as he broke bread
the blood was alive
was power
was energy
flowing into our hearts
to work to make
this a better world
there was an atmosphere of fear

as we passed into the city
that kills its prophets
could feel this fear
but it couldn't ever again
take over
my heart
i was different now
something had happened
i could never go back
to how
i was when i left yesterday
hurrying
to relate to friends
about this fire
strong
impelling

practical guidelines

The process that supports these meditations is both communal and individual. They can unroll during a liturgy or within a class. In either event, a worshiping community hears the Word of God; then the members of this community are led through a guided contemplation. The personal encounter with grace is then owned and appropriated within the community, so that the journey toward God is also a journey toward greater human solidarity.

A few concrete examples will illustrate this. The title of the meditation was "Freedom" (p. 48). On a Sunday in November at Juvenile Hall, after the reading of the Gospel, Dario called the young people to prayer. Two hundred heads bowed respectfully, postured to close out the cold reality of incarceration and readied to enter the scene that was about to be created. With a depth of feeling that came from his own possible prison future, Dario read the words of the meditation. One could feel the emotion, like a gentle rain falling on these young people, words about freedom heard by those considered to be worthless by society. The feeling that engulfed us was powerful and yet peaceful.

Dario read the words, and people listened and prayed, and were touched. Then three youths from the unit shared what had happened to them during the time of meditation. Over the years, they would have heard the witnessing of the born-again: the hard sell, the absolute certitude that leaves a vague feeling of discomfort. These three young men's language, with its simplicity and sincerity, was different from any type of religious hype. There was an austere beauty and a ripeness to the words in their attempt to articulate who God is for them. Some of them had been reflecting on these Gospel passages for more than six months in a meditation class. Their carefully chosen, judiciously pronounced words had a clarity and a comfort that communicated from heart to heart, drawing their listeners closer to God.

On another Sunday, Dario read the meditation on "Lepers" (p. 158). Afterward, Oscar shared how he could identify with the lepers. He talked about what it meant to be looked upon by others as an outcast because of his contact with gangs. Then Oscar shared how he too had met people who had shown him the same type of unconditional love that Jesus had shown to the leper in the Gospel scene. Could it be that God's unconditional love for these young people was made manifest during the weeks of meditation? Were the tears that flowed down the cheeks of many that day hints of God's presence, rumors of God's touch?

In a different place, and with a different crowd, there were similar results. I was with a group of eighth graders at Dolores Mission School, and we were meditating on our "handicaps." We used the meditation entitled "Zaccheus" (p. 165). The reflection touched upon the question, "Who really gets hurt when you 'bag' on someone who has some kind of deformity?" One youngster said that people who feel the love that Zaccheus did during the meditation wouldn't hurt one another as much as they do. The children talked about what the school would be like without them always "bagging" on each other.

As I experimented with this method in different pastoral situations, I wondered where the limits were. Once, while helping with a class on Ignatian spirituality at Loyola Marymount University, I was somewhat hesitant to use this dynamic, which, after all, had been developed at Juvenile Hall, in our grammar school, and among the people of our neighborhood. For some reason I ventured a try. The LMU students were surprisingly open to the experience. One of the women in the class was particularly touched by a meditation on the necessity of working as a team, entitled "Breakfast" (p. 226).

The joy and the sense of meaning that comes from the collective experience of working together is very different from the staid cycle of work, reward, and reputation. In the scene from "Breakfast," the people sitting around the fire were "compañeros." They had come back from the multifaceted encounters to be found in ministry. They were sharing their lives, their experiences, their views on what 'had happened,' reflecting on their lives and on the future. The fire around which they sat warmed not only hands and faces but hearts and souls. The bonds created were essential and sufficient for them to be able to follow in faithfulness the One who has gone before.

Another example of the use of these words is found in a meditation called "Fear" (p. 56). After a particular reading of this mediation, one seventh grader from the school shared how she was afraid to tell her mother how much she appreciates all that her mom does for her. Later that very week, her mother told me that her daughter had gone up to her, explained what had happened within her during the meditation, and said plainly how she loved her very much and was thankful for all her sacrifices to care for the family. This was a small but encouraging sign that something authentic was taking place. Somehow God was impelling this young one to take small steps toward great, life-transforming actions.

Love expressed, fear confessed, tenderness shared, fragility bared. The power of these words was made manifest too in death. During a Friday morning meditation on the words entitled "Deep Loss" (p. 108), in the little chapel upstairs in the school, death was embraced. Salvador had just lost one of his relatives. He talked about how he could feel the closeness of the dead person during the meditation. The next week he brought his daughter to the meditation so that she too could touch and be touched and thereby find something "more" in order to take strength during those difficult days of so much death.

Mondays we have a healing Mass in the afternoon. Put off by the circus of TV preachers, many people are today skeptical of God's healing power, especially in the hands of charlatans. We purposely choose to run the risk of their incredulity. The structure of the healing liturgy is very simple: a Scripture reading is followed by a meditation on healing, then the administration of the sacrament of the sick, during which two women from the parish pray over the sick person. We then proceed into the healing power which comes from the sharing of the Eucharist. Some of the meditations in this book were used during these healing liturgies. Some very moving stories emerged from the liturgies.

Finally, I would mention that these meditations have come to support in a very powerful way the Sunday liturgies at our parish. Had I not seen how these words could be used in a large group at Juvenile Hall, I would never have imagined using them on a Sunday at the church. In fact, they seem to work. Claudia, a woman from the neighborhood, said that she could feel a peace come to her during the time of meditation, that she felt closer to Jesus, and that something was calling her to be more.

My hope is that these words can be a tide that lifts us all higher. What Carlos said in the high-risk unit MN at Central Juvenile Hall perhaps says it all and says it best: "I was stressing out in the holding tank. I was very cold. I had not eaten for eight hours. I thought of meditating, and so I did for a while. My insides felt better."

reflection
questions

baptism

1. Can I remember an experience of being drawn to "I know not where," away from what I knew, away from what was comfortable? How did I feel?

2. Can I remember a moment of transformation? Is there a moment in my experience that changed my life, a moment in which I was freed from fear, a moment in which I knew God was with me? What was that like?

3. Where am I being led now? What in my life, in the world, am I "tired of seeing"? What would I like to change?

call

1. Do I have a dream? A dream that makes my heart beat faster, that gives me energy, gets me excited? Where does the call of the dream come from? Am I living that dream? Have I said yes to the dream?

2. What gives meaning to my life?

simplicity

1. How do I "give joy to the one who made all of this"?

2. Is there a time I can remember feeling like I was always running? When I wished I could slow down and walk? Is there a way to walk or to bask in my life as it is today?

3. Is my life complicated? Do I desire greater simplicity? "How do I get myself in the middle of such difficult situations?"

wedding

1. Who am I drawn to love? Where am I drawn to love?

2. Is God really seeking me? as a desirous bridegroom? as a jealous lover? In what ways have I experienced that love?

3. "Life is short." How is my life about love?

freedom

1. Is there someone I can bring hope to, be with in times of anguish?

2. Are there captives I can set free?

3. Am I holding captives?

4. How can I bring good news?

fear

1. Do I have a memory of a time when I kept my "eyes on Jesus"?

2. What prevents me from keeping my eyes on Jesus? Fear? Doubts? Do I need to do things my way?

3. Where do I feel fear? Where do I feel the need to be self-reliant?

matthew

1. Am I at peace with myself?

2. Does my life make sense?

3. Am I good enough to help Jesus with his work? How am I being asked to help? How do I respond to the invitation?

healing

1. How do I experience healing today?

2. For what do I desire healing?

prayer

1. How do I speak with "the one whom I love"?

2. What is my experience of speaking to and listening to God?

3. How can I keep the vision of the will of God? What is my part in the plan of God? What is God's dream for me?

nicodemus

1. Do I desire connection?

2. How do I feel the connection with all people? Are there those with whom I do not feel connected?

3. Is there a way that I separate myself from others? Do I feel superior, more important?

two by two

1. Is there love in my struggle to serve?

2. How am I changed by knowing Jesus?

3. Am I helping to prepare the way? Do I live knowing that Jesus is always with me? Can I heal the sick?

well

1. Can I go to the well of living water? How do I go there?

2. Is there anything in my well? Have I ever seen it? Do I visit it often for refreshment?

deep loss

1. How did I feel when David's heart started beating?

2. When did I experience Jesus bringing life into me, my family, my community?

3. Can I experience Jesus' presence in my deep sorrow?

storm

1. Do I lose my focus, feel overwhelmed by waves crashing in and filling my boat?

2. Do I take on too much? Do I lose my center, my ability to ride the unexpected waves?

3. What are the "stormlike states" in my own life? How can I choose more wisely — not creating unnecessary storms?

martha

1. Are there pains I hold deep within? the story of a death? a loss? my own humiliations? anger? shame?

2. Are there pains I need to share?

3. Can I let those out to Jesus, be present to the pain and to Jesus' presence, aware of all that is within me?

stones

1. When have I experienced injustice and hate?

2. Are there ways in which I hate myself?

3. Do I really believe that Jesus loves me unconditionally? that Jesus loves me even though he knows the parts of me that I deny or of which I am ashamed?

4. Are there ways I have numbed myself to my own pain? Is there pain in my life that I have hidden away so that I can survive? Can I bring this pain before Jesus?

humility

1. How do I feel when I bring myself before God?

2. Do I want to "own Yahweh"?

3. Do I believe "Yahweh seeks me out"? How do I experience that?

transfiguration

1. Do I know "deep mystery" in my life? What is it like? How does it feel?

2. "Deep mystery." Do I seek it? Does it come to me when I am not even trying?

3. Do I choose to put myself in the path of "deep mystery" — even if I fall asleep sometimes?

children

1. What did Jesus feel as he held and blessed the children? What did I feel as I watched Jesus with the children?

2. Can I imagine Jesus holding me and blessing me as he did the children? How does that feel?

lepers

1. Is there a part of my life that needs healing? Have I asked for that healing? Am I afraid to ask for that healing?

2. In what ways do I experience being an outcast? Are there parts of myself that I cast out? Do I believe Jesus can love those parts, can heal those parts?

3. Who are the outcasts in my world? Do I play a role in casting them out? Can I play a role in their healing?

zaccheus

1. Does my work have meaning? What do I hope to achieve in my work?

2. Are there those I look down on? Are there those I seek acceptance from?

3. How has Jesus' love changed me? How could Jesus' love change me?

pharisees

1. What do I most desire? Do I let other things get in the way of fulfilling this desire?

2. In what ways do I "rush by people in need"? How do I fulfill the law at the expense of meeting Jesus?

3. Are there parts of me that are crying out for help? Am I neglecting them in order to meet obligations?

multiplication

1. Is there a pain I have been carrying?

2. Are there experiences I have had that make me feel I have to rely on myself?

   3. Do I have gifts that I will not share out of fear and
      bitterness?

lazarus

   1. Do I live like "all this is not permanent, it is all so
      fleeting, we are on a pilgrimage"?

   2. In what ways do I try to hold on to this life rather
      than give it away?

   3. Am I open to "this other dimension of life," feeling
      how close the dead are to us? How do I experience
      that openness or its absence?

foot washing

   1. Can I remember a specific time when I was filled
      with Jesus' love? What was that like?

   2. In what ways do I "wash others' feet"? Am I able to
      let others "wash my feet"?

   3. How do I experience Jesus' love in my life at this
      moment?

agony

   1. What did I feel after reading the contemplation of
      Jesus' agony in the garden? When were other times I
      experienced those feelings?

   2. Have I experienced God's presence in a time when
      I thought I might "be destroyed by dark negative
      forces"? When was that time? What did I feel? Was
      I changed?

veronica

1. What were Veronica's feelings as she watched Jesus suffer and then made a small gesture to lessen his suffering? What were my feelings as I listened to her words?

2. Was there ever a time when I "knew what I needed to do" and did so, even though "the guards were approaching"? What did that feel like?

3. When have I experienced the power of Jesus' love in the face of suffering?

cross

1. Am I immersed in Jesus' struggle, "when people's lives are cracked open"?

2. How do I experience and respond to the emptiness that comes from suffering, loss, and death?

3. How do I experience the power that gets me through the struggle? How is that power lacking in my life?

breakfast

1. How am I bread broken for others? Who are those others? In what way do others allow themselves to be bread broken for me?

2. In what ways do I do the work of Jesus? With whom do I do the work?

3. Can I remember a time sharing a meal, being together with friends who do the work, knowing Jesus' peace and love in that experience?

emmaus

1. Do I experience "the blood flowing in my life, the connection to all who enter the struggle"?

2. What makes my heart feel excited? What gives meaning and energy and renews my faith?

3. Where in my life do I see Jesus in the breaking of the bread? What are the simple things that reveal Jesus in my life?

further reading on ignatian spirituality

Barry, William A., S.J. *Finding God in All Things: A Companion to the Spiritual Exercises of St. Ignatius.* Notre Dame, Ind.: Ave Maria Press, 1991.

Fleming, David L., S.J. *Draw Me into Your Friendship: The Spiritual Exercises (A Literal Translation and a Contemporary Reading).* St. Louis: The Institute of Jesuit Sources, 1996.

Harbaugh, Jim, S.J. *A 12-Step Approach to the Spiritual Exercises of St. Ignatius.* Kansas City, Mo.: Sheed & Ward, 1997.

Lonsdale, David, S.J. *Eyes to See, Ears to Hear: An Introduction to Ignatian Spirituality.* Chicago: Loyola University Press, 1990.

———. *Listening to the Music of the Spirit: The Art of Discernment.* Notre Dame, Ind.: Ave Maria Press, 1992.